THE
ASIAN
KITCHEN

THE
A
S
I
A
N
KITCHEN

✳

70 RECIPES FOR
POPULAR DISHES,
FROM DUMPLINGS
AND NOODLE SOUPS
TO STIR-FRIES AND
RICE BOWLS

RYLAND PETERS & SMALL
LONDON • NEW YORK

Designer Paul Stradling
Editor Emily Calder
Head of Production Patricia Harrington
Creative Director Leslie Harrington
Editorial Director Julia Charles

Indexer Vanessa Bird
Proofreader Kate Reeves-Brown

First published in 2022 by Ryland Peters & Small
20–21 Jockey's Fields
London WC1R 4BW
and
341 E 116th St
New York, NY 10029

www.rylandpeters.com

10 9 8 7 6 5 4 3 2 1

Recipe collection compiled by Emily Calder.
Text ©Valerie Aikman-Smith, Nadia Arumagum,
Ghillie Basan, Vatcharin Bhumichitr, James Campbell,
Ross Dobson, Mat Follas, Liz Franklin, Tonia George,
Brian Glover, Carol Hilker, Atsuko Ikeda, Kathy
Kordalis, Loretta Liu, Uyen Luu, Dan May, Louise
Pickford, Annie Rigg, Laura Santini, Leah Vanderveldt,
Laura Washburn Hutton, Belinda Williams 2022.

Design and photographs © Ryland Peters & Small
2022 (see page 144 for photo credits).

ISBN: 978-1-78879-436-7

A CIP record for this book is available from
the British Library.
US Library of Congress Cataloging-in-
Publication Data has been applied for.

Printed and bound in China.

NOTES

• Both British (metric) and American (imperial plus US cups) are included in these recipes for your convenience; however it is important to work with one set of measurements and not alternate between the two within a recipe.

• All spoon measurements are level unless otherwise specified.

• All eggs are medium (UK) or large (US), unless otherwise specified. Uncooked or partially cooked eggs should not be served to the very old, frail, young children, pregnant women or those with compromised immune systems.

• When a recipe calls for the grated zest of citrus fruit, buy unwaxed fruit and wash well before using. If you can only find treated fruit, scrub well in warm soapy water before using.

• Ovens should be preheated to the specified temperatures. We recommend using an oven thermometer. If using a fan-assisted oven, adjust temperatures according to the manufacturer's instructions.

CONTENTS

INTRODUCTION

The foods of East and Southeast Asia are amongst the freshest, most vibrant, and most flavoursome in the world. Not only are they delicious, healthy, and bursting with taste, but as densely populated regions they provide a huge variety of unique cuisines, including Thai, Vietnamese, Japanese and Korean. The geographical and historical influences of the flavours involved means that these recipes provide a melting pot of textures and tastes.

The Asian Kitchen prizes tender meats and fiery sauces which make the most of the fascinating local flavours found in the relevant regions. These cuisines are also naturally abundant in vegetables; making many of these recipes ideal for vegetarians and vegans who want to enjoy the lively aromas of Asian food without missing out on flavours. From creamy curries from Thailand, to rich and hearty noodle dishes from Vietnam, all these dishes are equally delicious. The recipes pack in all of the most distinctive and notable Asian flavours, with tasty notes of miso, fragrant spices and aromatic herbs, the unique essence of lemon grass, peppery tastes, thick noodles, and everything that is delicious, healthy and comforting about these cuisines.

This book brings 70 recipes for dressings, pastes and dipping sauces, small bites, soups, noodles and rice, curries and stews, main plates and sweet things which embrace all the classic flavours and key dishes from East and Southeast Asian countries. Those keen to jump into playing with flavours will enjoy whipping up Fresh Curry Pastes and Dipping Sauces from scratch, whilst anyone looking for a nourishing nibble will love classic Spring Rolls, rich Barbecue Pork Bao and crunchy Sesame Prawn Toasts with Pickled Carrot. Cold winter evenings will welcome in the comfort of Chicken Noodle Soup, and satisfyingly-slurpy Peppered Beef Pho, whilst hot afternoons will be perfect for carby classics like Beef Chow Mein, or an Egg-Fried Rice to use up those leftover summer veggies. Dinners with friends will be excellently catered for with flavoursome staples like Green Coconut Shrimp Curry. Finish off the meal with a variety of sweet dishes, including the Thai staple Sticky Rice with Mango and the much-treasured Hong Kong Egg Tart.

CHAPTER ☀ 1

DRESSINGS, PASTES & DIPPING SAUCES

GREEN CURRY PASTE

TO MAKE A PROPER THAI GREEN CURRY, THE GREEN CURRY PASTE MUST
BE AUTHENTIC. THE ONE BELOW IS SIMPLE TO MAKE AND WILL KEEP WELL
IN THE FRIDGE FOR SEVERAL WEEKS. THIS IS AN ESSENTIAL INGREDIENT
IN THE RECIPE FOR GREEN THAI SOUP (PAGE 55).

1 teaspoon coriander seeds

½ teaspoon cumin seeds

6 white peppercorns

3 large green chillies/chiles,
   deseeded and sliced

4 green bird's-eye chillies/
   chiles, deseeded and sliced

4 spring onions/scallions, thinly
   sliced on a diagonal

4 garlic cloves, peeled

2.5-cm/1-in. piece of galangal,
   peeled and sliced

4 freshly chopped coriander/
   cilantro stalks, roots included

1 lemongrass stalk, trimmed

2 teaspoons shrimp paste

4 teaspoons groundnut/
   peanut oil

MAKES 150 ML/⅔ CUP

Dry-fry the coriander seeds, cumin seeds and peppercorns
until they turn golden and begin to release their aroma. Leave
to cool, then grind to a powder in a spice grinder.

Put all the chillies, the spring onions, garlic, galangal, fresh
coriander, lemongrass, shrimp paste and oil in a food processor
or blender and process to form a smooth paste. Transfer
to a bowl and stir in the ground spices. Store in a sterilized,
screwtop jar in the fridge and use as directed by the recipe.

RED CURRY PASTE

THIS MAY LOOK LIKE HARD WORK WITH THE LIST OF INGREDIENTS, BUT ONCE YOU HAVE MADE THIS PASTE YOU CAN STORE IT IN THE FRIDGE FOR A WEEK. IT'S FIERY AND FILLED WITH AROMATICS, BUT ONCE YOU ADD IT TO COCONUT MILK FOR A CURRY IT BECOMES A WONDERFUL CREAMY SAUCE.

2 tablespoons fresh ginger, peeled and grated

6 red fresh chillies/chiles, deseeded and sliced

4 bird's eye chillies/chiles, deseeded and sliced

6 lime leaves, roughly chopped

1 lemongrass stalk, roughly chopped

4 garlic cloves, minced

2 teaspoons sambal selek (Asian chilli/chile paste)

2 tablespoons fish sauce

1 teaspoon shrimp paste

freshly squeezed juice and grated zest of 1 lime

1 teaspoon palm sugar/jaggery

2 tablespoons vegetable oil

MAKES SCANT 180 ML/¾ CUP

Put all the ingredients in a food processor or blender and process to a coarse paste.

Store the paste in an airtight container in the fridge for up to 1 week.

Use to spice up curries, soups, or in a dressing for an Asian salad, or rub onto fish and allow to marinate before cooking as preferred.

CHINESE DIPPING SAUCE

A PERFECT SAUCE FOR STEAMED OR FRIED WONTONS AND ALL KINDS OF NOODLE DISHES.

50 ml/scant ¼ cup light soy sauce

2 teaspoons Chinese black vinegar

1 teaspoon caster/granulated sugar

1 teaspoon fresh ginger, peeled and grated

1 teaspoon sesame oil

¼ teaspoon chilli/chile oil

sterilized glass jar with airtight lid

MAKES 75 ML/⅓ CUP

Whisk all the ingredients together in a bowl, or, if you have a clean glass jar with a lid, put all the ingredients into the jar, screw on the lid and shake well.

Serve immediately or store in a glass jar with an airtight lid in the fridge. The sauce will keep for up to 5 days.

JAPANESE DIPPING SAUCE

TRADITIONALLY SERVED IN HOT SUMMER MONTHS WITH CHILLED NOODLES.

200 ml/¾ cup dashi broth (see right)

3 tablespoons Japanese soy sauce

3 tablespoons mirin

½ teaspoon caster/granulated sugar

sterilized glass jar with airtight lid

MAKES 300 ML/1¼ CUPS

FOR THE DASHI BROTH

15 g/1 tablespoon chopped dried kombu

15 g/1 tablespoon dried bonito flakes

MAKES 1 LITRE/QUART

For the dashi broth, pour 1.25 litres/1¼ quarts cold water into a saucepan, add the kombu and set aside for 30 minutes to soften. Bring the mixture to the boil over a medium heat, removing any scum that appears on the surface, then reduce the heat and simmer gently for 10 minutes. Remove the pan from the heat, stir in the bonito flakes and allow the broth to cool. Strain with a fine mesh sieve/strainer and use immediately or chill until required. The broth will keep stored in an airtight container for 3 days in the fridge or can be frozen for up to 1 month.

Tip: For a vegetarian option, omit the bonito flakes and increase the kombu to a total of 20 g/1½ tablespoons.

For the dipping sauce, whisk all the ingredients together in a bowl, or, if you have a clean glass jar with a lid, put all the ingredients into the jar, screw on the lid and shake well. Serve immediately or store in a glass jar with an airtight lid in the fridge. You can store the sauce in the fridge for up to 3 days.

KOREAN DIPPING SAUCES

KOREA IS FAMED FOR ITS LOVE OF THE CONDIMENT OR SIDE DISH. CHOGANJANG IS THE SIMPLEST OF DIPPING SAUCES, PERFECT WITH ALL NOODLE DISHES. IF YOU PREFER YOUR SAUCES SPICY, TRY CHO-GOCHUJANG. SSAMJANG IS A SPICY FERMENTED CHILLI/CHILE BEAN PASTE, OFTEN SERVED WITH KOREAN BBQ, BUT ALSO DELICIOUS STIRRED INTO KOREAN SOUPS.

CHOGANJANG

a pinch of sesame seeds
2 tablespoons dark soy sauce
1 tablespoon brown rice vinegar

MAKES 45 ML/3 TABLESPOONS

Dry-fry the sesame seeds in a small frying pan/skillet set over a medium heat until evenly toasted. Pour the soy sauce and vinegar into a small bowl and sprinkle with a few sesame seeds.

Use as required or store the soy and vinegar mixture without the sesame seeds in a sterilized glass bottle until ready to serve.

CHO-GOCHUJANG

1 tablespoon sesame seeds
1–2 teaspoons gochujang
2 tablespoons rice wine vinegar
2 tablespoons dark soy sauce
1 tablespoon runny honey
2 teaspoons sesame oil
1 spring onion/scallion, thinly sliced on a diagonal
1 garlic clove, minced

MAKES 150 ML/⅔ CUP

Dry-fry the sesame seeds in a small frying pan/skillet set over a medium heat until evenly toasted. Transfer to a spice grinder or pestle and mortar and grind to a rough paste.

Put the ground sesame seeds in a small bowl and stir in the gochujang, vinegar, soy sauce, honey and sesame oil until smooth, then add the spring onion and garlic and stir well. Serve immediately.

SSAMJANG

1 teaspoon sesame seeds
60 ml/¼ cup doenjang
2 teaspoons gochujang
1 spring onion/scallion, thinly sliced on a diagonal
1 small garlic clove, minced
1 Asian shallot, finely chopped
2 teaspoons rice wine
2 teaspoons sesame oil
1 teaspoon runny honey

MAKES 150 ML/⅔ CUP

Dry-fry the sesame seeds in a small frying pan/skillet set over a medium heat until evenly toasted. Put all the ingredients in a small bowl and use as required.

Alternatively, transfer to a plastic container, seal and store in the fridge for up to 3 days.

NUOC CHAM
(VIETNAMESE-STYLE DIPPING SAUCE) *[left]*

VIETNAMESE CUISINE IS ONE OF THE MOST INTERESTING AND DIVERSE IN THE WORLD. NUOC CHAM AND ITS VARIATIONS ARE NOW PERHAPS ITS MOST UNIVERSALLY AVAILABLE SAUCE AND ARE ADDED AS REQUIRED TO VIRTUALLY ANY SAVOURY DISH. IT IS PARTICULARLY GOOD WHEN DRIZZLED OVER RICE DISHES OR AS A DIP FOR VEGETABLE TEMPURA.

1 small lime
3 garlic cloves, minced
2 small hot green chillies/chiles, deseeded and sliced
4 teaspoons caster/granulated sugar
60 ml/¼ cup Vietnamese-style fish sauce

MAKES 150 ML/⅔ CUP

Squeeze the juice from the lime into a small bowl and set aside. Scrape the pulp from the lime and grind it, along with the garlic and chillies, with a pestle and mortar to form a paste. If you find it difficult to get a paste, the ingredients could be briefly pulsed in a food processor or blender.

Add 75 ml/⅓ cup water and the sugar to the bowl of lime juice and stir until the sugar has dissolved. Scrape the chilli paste into the bowl, add the fish sauce and mix well.

Vietnamese fish sauce is lighter in style than traditional Nam Pla (Thai fish sauce). If you are unable to source this, Thai-style fish sauce still works well but you may wish to reduce the quantity slightly or add to taste.

PEA & WASABI DIP

A QUICK RECIPE THAT MAKES USE OF THE FREEZER AND STORE CUPBOARD TO WHIP UP A FRESH AND SPICY DIP PERFECT FOR AFTERNOON SNACKING.

½ small red onion, finely diced
white wine vinegar, to cover
150 g/1¼ cups frozen peas, slightly defrosted
1 teaspoon wasabi powder
1 teaspoon light soy sauce
grated zest of 1 lemon
a pinch of salt, to season
fresh vegetable sticks or cheese crackers, to serve

MAKES 350 ML/1½ CUPS

Put the onion in a small bowl and just cover with the vinegar. Set aside to infuse for 15 minutes.

Put the peas, wasabi, soy and lemon zest in a jug/pitcher of about 300-ml/10-oz. capacity that is only slightly larger in diameter than the blade end of a handheld electric blender. Purée the contents to make a smooth, thick paste. Taste and, if you like your dip hotter, add a little more wasabi, then blend again.

Add a heaped teaspoon of drained red onion pieces and a good pinch of table salt. Mix together with a spoon.

Serve as a dip with fresh vegetable sticks, or on crackers.

SWEET CHILLI/CHILE SAUCE

THIS IS A CASE OF 'LESS IS MORE'. THE RECIPE USES INGREDIENTS YOU'VE PROBABLY ALREADY GOT IN YOUR STORE CUPBOARD. WHEN YOU USE FRESH INGREDIENTS, ALTHOUGH THEY MAY LIMIT THE SHELF-LIFE, THEY PRODUCE A FRESH, DELICIOUS AND SIMPLE SAUCE. YOU'LL NEVER BUY SWEET CHILLI/ CHILE SAUCE AGAIN.

2 red bird's eye chillies/chiles, deseeded and sliced

250 ml/1 cup white wine vinegar

250 g/1¼ cup caster/granulated sugar

2 garlic cloves, minced

MAKES 350 ML/1½ CUPS

Place the chillies, vinegar and sugar in a saucepan. Set over a medium heat, bring to a simmer and continue to simmer until the volume has reduced by half. Remove the pan from the heat and leave to cool for about 5 minutes.

Add the garlic and stir to combine. Set aside for at least 15 minutes, to allow to cool and the flavours to infuse.

Use immediately or store in an airtight container in the fridge for up to 6 weeks. The mixture can become quite thick when it cools down, so do not store it in a bottle.

Note: The cooking of this sauce comes with a health warning. If you are tempted to speed-up the process by turning the heat up too high, the chillies and vinegar fumes are fierce, to say the least, so a low simmer and good ventilation are needed.

Do not be tempted to add the garlic any earlier than stated in the recipe. In boiling vinegar, garlic turns green; it still tastes good but will not look as appetizing!

KOREAN MARINADE

THIS IS ONE OF THOSE MARINADES YOU CAN MAKE OVER AND OVER AGAIN
AND NEVER TIRE OF. USE IT ON RIBS AND FIRE UP THE GRILL.

80 ml/⅓ cup vegetable oil

80 ml/⅓ cup soy sauce

60 ml/¼ cup toasted sesame oil

3 tablespoons sherry

4 tablespoons brown sugar

3 tablespoons curry powder

2 tablespoons fresh ginger,
   peeled and grated

4 garlic cloves, minced

3 spring onions/scallions, thinly
   sliced on a diagonal

salt and freshly ground black
   pepper, to season

MAKES 360 ML/1½ CUPS

Put all the ingredients except for the salt and pepper
in a blender or food processor and process until blended,
then season with salt and pepper.

Store the marinade in an airtight container in the fridge for
up to 10 days.

To use, put the meat in a ceramic dish, pour over the marinade
and leave to marinate for 8–24 hours in the fridge. Let the meat
come to room temperature, then cook as preferred. This
marinade can be used on ribs, chicken, pork, tofu and lamb.

CHAPTER
☀
2

CHINESE POT STICKERS

NOT TO BE CONFUSED WITH WONTONS, POT STICKERS, AS THEY ARE CALLED IN NORTH AMERICA, ARE A FORM OF CHINESE DUMPLING THAT IS FRIED, STEAMED AND THEN FRIED AGAIN SO THEY ARE AT ONCE BOTH SOFT AND CRISPY. IT'S BEST TO USE A NON-STICK FRYING PAN/SKILLET TO MAKE THESE RATHER THAN A WOK AS YOU NEED AN EVEN BASE FOR THE OIL TO SETTLE.

125 g/2 cups finely chopped Chinese cabbage

1 teaspoon salt

1 leek, trimmed and finely chopped

2 garlic cloves, minced

2 tablespoons freshly chopped coriander/cilantro

250 g/1 cup minced/ground pork

24 gyoza wrappers

2 tablespoons vegetable oil

1 quantity dipping sauce of choice

garlic chive flowers, to garnish (optional)

a baking sheet lined with baking parchment

SERVES 4

Put the cabbage in a large mixing bowl with the salt and toss well to coat. Transfer to a colander and leave to drain for 1 hour to remove as much water as possible from the cabbage. Squeeze out any remaining water and put the cabbage in a clean large mixing bowl with the leek, garlic and coriander. Gradually work in the minced pork until combined.

Working one at a time, lay the gyoza wrappers out flat and place a teaspoon of the mixture on one half of each wrapper. Dampen the edges with a little cold water, fold the wrapper over the filling and carefully press the edges together to seal.

Preheat the oven to 110°C (225°F) Gas ¼ (or the lowest heat setting).

Heat 1 tablespoon of the oil in a wok or large non-stick frying pan/skillet set over a high heat. Add half the dumplings and fry for about 1 minute until the bottoms are golden. Add 100 ml/scant ½ cup water and simmer, partially covered, for 5 minutes, until the water has evaporated. Cook for a further 2–3 minutes until the bottoms are crispy.

Transfer the dumplings to the prepared baking sheet, turn off the oven and set in the still-warm oven while you cook the remaining dumplings in the same way.

Arrange the dumplings on plates and serve drizzled with the dipping sauce. Garnish with garlic chive flowers, if wished, and serve.

VEGETARIAN SPRING ROLLS

SPRING ROLLS ARE A DELICIOUS AND TIMELESS CLASSIC, AND THESE ARE
GREAT SERVED WITH FRIENDS AS A DELICIOUS SNACK, APPETIZER OR SIDE.

15 g/⅔ cup tree ear
   mushrooms/dried black cloud
   ear fungus

25 g/1 oz. cellophane noodles

75 g/3 oz. carrots

50 g/a small handful of
   mangetouts/snow peas

1 tablespoon vegetable oil

1 teaspoon fresh ginger, peeled
   and grated

25 g/scant ½ cup spinach, torn

1 tablespoon light or dark soy
   sauce

1 tablespoon oyster sauce

a pinch of freshly ground black
   pepper, to season

16 large spring roll wrappers

1–2 eggs, lightly beaten

Sweet Chilli/Chile sauce,
   to serve (page 16)

a baking sheet lined with baking
   parchment

SERVES 4

Put the mushrooms in a large mixing bowl, cover with boiling water and soak for 20 minutes until softened. Drain well, pat dry with paper towels and slice thinly, discarding any tough stalks. Set aside.

Meanwhile, put the noodles in a bowl, cover with boiling water and soak for 30 minutes until softened. Drain the noodles and pat dry with paper towels. Using scissors, cut the noodles into 5-cm/2-in. lengths and set aside.

Cut the carrots into 5-cm/2-in. batons and the mangetouts into similar-sized shreds.

Heat the oil in a wok or large frying pan/skillet and stir-fry the ginger for a few seconds before adding the carrots and mangetouts. Stir-fry for 2 minutes before adding the mushrooms, spinach, soy sauce, oyster sauce and black pepper. Stir well and remove the pan from the heat. Stir in the noodles and set aside to cool completely.

Working one wrapper at a time, trim each to 12 x 18 cm/4¾ x 7 in., lay out flat and brush the top with beaten egg. Place a tablespoon of the cooled filling in a log shape along one edge of the wrapper. Roll over once, then fold the ends in and over the roll. Continue to roll up tightly to form a sealed parcel.

Preheat the oven to 110°C (225°F) Gas ¼, or the lowest heat setting.

Pour vegetable oil into a wok or large saucepan to reach about 5 cm/2 in. up the side and set over a medium–high heat. Heat until a cube of bread dropped into the oil crisps in 30 seconds. Deep-fry the rolls a few at a time for 1–2 minutes until crisp and golden. Drain on paper towels and transfer the rolls to the prepared baking sheet. Turn off the oven and set in the still-warm oven while you cook the remaining rolls in the same way.

Serve the spring rolls hot with sweet chilli sauce.

STEAMED RICE NOODLE DUMPLINGS WITH SCALLOPS

DIM SUM OR 'YUM CHA', AS IT'S KNOWN IN AUSTRALIA, IS ALWAYS A DELICIOUS LUNCH OR SIDE.

250 g/½ lb. scallops (without corals)

50 g/1½ oz. (about 6) water chestnuts, drained and chopped

2 garlic cloves, minced

1 tablespoon freshly chopped garlic chives

1 tablespoon light soy sauce

2 teaspoons oyster sauce

1 teaspoon sesame oil

24 wonton wrappers

3–4 tablespoons sunflower/safflower oil

Asian dressing of choice

spring onions/scallions, thinly sliced on a diagonal, to garnish

a baking sheet lined with baking parchment

a medium bamboo steamer

SERVES 4

Begin by preparing the scallops, cutting away the grey muscle attached at one side and chopping into small cubes. Put the scallop meat into a bowl with the chestnuts, garlic, garlic chives, soy sauce, oyster sauce and sesame oil, and stir.

Lay the wonton wrappers flat on a board and place a teaspoon of the scallop mixture in the centre. Brush around the edges with a little water and draw the sides up and around the filling, pressing the edges together to seal. Transfer each one to the prepared baking sheet.

Dip the base of each dumpling in sunflower oil and transfer to the bamboo steamer. Cover and steam over a pan of simmering water for 10–12 minutes until firm and cooked through.

Serve with the dressing, garnished with spring onions.

(See image, front cover)

EGG ROLLS

THERE IS SOMETHING SO SATISFYING ABOUT AN EGG ROLL. MAYBE IT'S THE CRUNCH; MAYBE IT'S THE TEXTURE; MAYBE IT'S SOMETHING ABOUT HOW PORK AND CABBAGE COME TOGETHER SO WELL WHEN HUGGED BETWEEN EGG ROLL WRAPPERS AND DEEP FRIED. WHATEVER IT IS, THEY'RE DELICIOUS!

3 tablespoons olive oil

1 teaspoon salt

1 teaspoon freshly ground black pepper

1 teaspoon ground ginger

1 teaspoon garlic powder

450 g/1 lb. pork shoulder

1 litre/quart groundnut/peanut oil, for frying

2 tablespoons plain/all-purpose flour

2 tablespoons water

120 g/2 cups cabbage, shredded

1 medium carrot, shredded

8 x 18-cm/7-in. square egg roll wrappers

2 tablespoons sesame seeds (optional)

FOR THE SWEET AND SOUR SAUCE

1 tablespoon soy sauce

1 tablespoon water

3½ tablespoons caster/granulated sugar

3½ tablespoons white vinegar

zest of 1 unwaxed orange

meat thermometer

MAKES 8

Preheat an oven to 180°C (350°F) Gas 4.

Spread the oil, salt, ground black pepper, ginger and garlic powder on the pork shoulder.

Set the meat on a rack set into a roasting pan. Roast for 20 minutes, and then reduce the heat to 160°C (325°F) Gas 3. Continue to cook until an instant-read thermometer inserted into the shoulder reads 85°C (185°F), about 1–2 hours. Remove the pork from the oven and let stand until cool enough to handle, about 30 minutes. Shred the pork.

Combine the flour and water in a bowl until they form a paste. In a separate bowl combine the cabbage, carrots and shredded pork and mix them together.

Lay out one egg roll wrapper with a corner pointed toward you. Place about 20 g/¼ cup of the cabbage, carrot and shredded pork mixture onto the wrapper and fold the corner up over the mixture. Fold the left and right corners toward the centre and continue to roll. Brush a bit of the flour paste on the final corner to help seal.

In a large frying pan/skillet, heat the oil to about 190°C (375°F). Place the egg rolls into the heated oil and fry, turning occasionally, until golden brown. Remove from the oil and drain on paper towels or a wire rack. Put on a serving plate and top with sesame seeds if desired.

To make the sweet and sour sauce, mix all the ingredients together in a mixing bowl. Transfer to a small saucepan and bring to the boil, then remove from the heat. Pour the sauce into a small bowl ready for dipping.

SUMMER ROLLS

THESE REFRESHING, FRAGRANT ROLLS ARE THE PERFECT ACCOMPANIMENT
TO MANY RECIPES IN THIS BOOK.

60 g/2 oz. rice vermicelli

8 rice wrappers (22-cm/8½-in. diameter)

3 tablespoons freshly chopped mint leaves

3 tablespoons freshly chopped coriander/cilantro

2 lettuce leaves, chopped

1½ tablespoons fish sauce

2 tablespoons freshly squeezed lime juice

2 garlic cloves, minced

1½ tablespoons caster/granulated sugar

½ teaspoon Sweet Chilli/Chile Sauce (page 16)

2 tablespoons hoisin sauce

1 teaspoon finely chopped peanuts

MAKES 8

Bring a medium saucepan of water to boil. Boil the rice vermicelli for 3–5 minutes, or until al dente, and drain.

Fill a large bowl with warm water. Dip one rice wrapper into the water for 1 second to soften. Lay the wrapper flat. In a row across the centre, place a handful of vermicelli, mint, coriander and lettuce, leaving about 5 cm/2 in. uncovered on each side. Fold the uncovered sides inward, then tightly roll the wrapper, beginning at the end with the lettuce. Repeat with remaining ingredients.

In a small bowl, mix the fish sauce, 4 tablespoons water, lime juice, garlic, sugar and chilli sauce. In another small bowl, mix the hoisin sauce and peanuts. Serve immediately with the summer rolls.

KAKIAGE PANCAKES

KAKIAGE PANCAKES ARE A VERY SIMPLE YET COMFORTING AND DELICIOUS STREET-FOOD FOUND ALL OVER JAPAN. THEY MUST BE SERVED FRESHLY COOKED TO RETAIN THEIR CRISPNESS AND THE COATING OF BATTER ONLY NEEDS TO BE EXTREMELY LIGHT.

200 g/1½ cups self-raising/ self-rising flour

200 g/2 cups cornflour/ cornstarch

large pinch of salt, to season

approx. 400–500 ml/1¾ –2 cups very cold sparkling water

1 red onion

1 carrot

burdock root (or salsify is a nice alternative)

a small bunch of spring onions/ scallions

1 sweet potato

vegetable oil, for deep-frying

ponzu sauce (store-bought), for dipping

MAKES 10–15

To make the pancake batter, put the dry ingredients into a large mixing bowl and slowly whisk in the very cold sparkling water until you get a nice smooth, thick pancake batter with a dropping consistency. To make the vegetable filling, peel (as necessary) and slice your chosen vegetables into fine strips. Place the vegetables in a large bowl and mix with just enough batter to bind them all together.

Preheat the vegetable oil in a deep-fryer to 180°C (350°F) or fill a large heavy-based pan half-full with vegetable oil and heat until a cube of bread sizzles and rises to the surface instantly. Dip a dessert spoon briefly into the hot oil then pick up a portion of the battered vegetables with the same spoon and drop it carefully into the fryer.

Cook a few pancakes at a time for approximately 2–3 minutes until golden, turning halfway. Remove with a slotted spoon and drain on paper towels. Repeat with the remaining batter and serve the hot pancakes immediately with ponzu sauce or any Asian dipping sauce.

BARBECUE PORK BAO

THE PILLOWY-SOFT BREAD BUN SURROUNDING SWEET AND STICKY
CHAR SIU-STYLE PORK IS JUST A HEAVENLY COMBINATION.

1 batch bread dough (see below)

1 tablespoon sunflower oil

1 shallot, chopped

2 tablespoons dry sherry

350 g/12 oz. pork loin, diced

1 teaspoon garlic, minced

2 tablespoons runny honey

2 tablespoons hoisin sauce

1 teaspoon Chinese five-spice
powder

1 tablespoon soy sauce

FOR THE BREAD DOUGH

2 teaspoons dry easy-bake yeast

450 g/3½ cups Asian white
wheat flour

100 g/¾ cup plus 1 tablespoon
icing sugar/confectioners'
sugar, sifted

15 g/2 tablespoons dried milk
powder

¼ teaspoon salt

2 teaspoons baking powder

50 ml/scant ¼ cup vegetable oil,
plus extra for oiling the bowl

a bamboo steamer, lined with
parchment paper

MAKES 16

Place the yeast in a large mixing bowl, then add the flour, sugar, milk powder, salt and baking powder. Make sure the yeast is separated from the salt by the layer of flour. Add the water and oil and bring together with a dough scraper. When no dry flour remains, remove the dough from the bowl and place on a lightly floured surface. Knead firmly for 5–10 minutes, until smooth and elastic. Lightly oil the mixing bowl. Shape the dough into two cylinders and place back in the oiled bowl, cover with oiled clingfilm/plastic wrap and leave in a warm place to rise for 40–60 minutes or until doubled in size.

To make the filling, heat the oil in a flameproof casserole dish and add the shallot. Cook over a medium heat until lightly caramelized, about 5–7 minutes. Pour in the sherry and let the alcohol cook out for a few minutes. Lower the heat a little and add the pork. Cook, stirring, for a further 2 minutes or until lightly browned.

Meanwhile, in a separate bowl mix the garlic, honey, hoisin sauce, Chinese five-spice powder and soy sauce with 2 tablespoons of water. Add this to the pork and shallot mixture. Stir well. Cover and cook over a low heat for 1 hour or until the sauce has thickened and the pork is tender. Add a little extra water if necessary. Remove the risen dough from the bowl, punch it down and knead it again briefly. Roll the dough out into a big rectangle and portion it out into 16 equal balls. Cover the dough balls with oiled clingfilm/plastic wrap and leave to rest again for 30 minutes in a warm place. Roll out each dough ball so that it has a diameter of around 7.5 cm/3 inches; try to make the centre slightly thicker than the edges. Place a heaped tablespoon of filling in the centre of each round. Gather the edges to form pleats and pinch to seal the top of the bun. Set the buns into a lined bamboo steamer at least 5 cm/2 in. apart. Cover with oiled clingfilm/plastic wrap and allow to rise for 30 minutes. Steam the buns over boiling water for 8–10 minutes until the dough is fluffy. Let cool slightly and serve.

MIXED SASHIMI

THIS PRETTY SASHIMI WITH GINGER SOY DRESSING AND MICRO HERB GARNISH USES SALMON AND TUNA. ASK YOUR FISHMONGER FOR THE VERY BEST, FRESHEST FISH HE HAS TO OFFER. IF YOU PREFER, YOU CAN SEAR THE FISH QUICKLY IN A SMOKING-HOT FRYING PAN/SKILLET.

250 g/9 oz. sushi-grade tuna fillet

250 g/9 oz. skinless salmon fillet, pin bones removed

5-cm/2-in. piece of mooli/ daikon radish

4 red-skinned radishes, trimmed

4 spring onions/scallions, thinly sliced on a diagonal

1 tablespoon pickled ginger

micro herbs, baby rocket/ arugula, or fresh coriander/ cilantro

FOR THE GINGER SOY DRESSING

½ fresh red chilli/chile, deseeded and sliced

½–1 teaspoon wasabi paste

2 tablespoons soy sauce

freshly squeezed juice of ½ a lime

SERVES 4

Cut the fish into thin slices and arrange on a platter.

Peel and cut the mooli into fine matchsticks. Cut the radishes into fine matchsticks. Mix the mooli, radishes and spring onions together and add to the platter. Add the pickled ginger, too.

To make the ginger soy dressing, mix together the chopped chilli, wasabi paste, soy sauce and lime juice in a little bowl.

Garnish the sashimi with the micro herbs and serve immediately with the ginger soy dressing.

TRADITIONAL PRAWN/SHRIMP DUMPLINGS (GAO)

ALSO KNOWN AS HAR GAO, THESE LITTLE DUMPLINGS ARE ONE OF THE MOST ICONIC DIM SUM DISHES.

50 g/1¾ oz. firm tofu, drained and minced

150 g/5½ oz. uncooked prawns/shrimp, shelled and deveined

1 teaspoon fresh ginger, peeled and grated

1 teaspoon minced garlic

½ teaspoon Shaoxing rice wine

½ teaspoon salt

½ teaspoon caster/granulated sugar

½ teaspoon ground white pepper

1 teaspoon olive oil

1 teaspoon cornflour/cornstarch

FOR THE CRYSTAL SKIN DOUGH

100 g/¾ cup wheat starch

50 g/½ cup tapioca starch

a pinch of salt

150 ml/⅔ cup boiling (not hot) water

FOR THE DIPPING SAUCE

1 small piece fresh ginger, peeled and grated

6 tablespoons black vinegar

a bamboo steamer lined with parchment paper

MAKES 16

Squeeze out the excess water from the tofu and finely mince using a sharp knife. Chop each prawn into 4–5 small pieces and place in a bowl. Add the drained and minced tofu, ginger, garlic, Shaoxing rice wine, salt, sugar, white pepper, oil, and cornflour. Mix well and set aside in the fridge to marinate while you make the dough.

For the dough, in a large mixing bowl, combine the wheat starch, tapioca starch and salt. Add the boiling water and mix with a wooden spoon until a dough is formed. Transfer to a lightly floured surface and knead until smooth. Separate the dough in half and roll into two equal cylinders, about 2.5 cm/1 in. diameter. Wrap in clingfilm/plastic wrap and rest until needed.

Divide the dough into 16 equal balls. On a lightly floured surface use a rolling pin to flatten the dough balls into thin discs, about 5 cm/2 in. diameter. Cover the finished skins with a damp kitchen cloth as you work so that they don't dry out.

Place a large teaspoon of filling neatly into the centre of a skin. Fold the skin in half over the filling. Pinch one end together and start to crimp the edge by making small folds to form pleats to create the traditional crescent shape.

Put the dumplings into the bamboo steamer lined with parchment paper. Steam over boiling water for 15–20 minutes or until the skin is transparent and the prawns are pink.

To make the dipping sauce, stir the minced ginger into the black vinegar. Serve the dumplings hot alongside the dipping sauce.

SESAME PRAWN/SHRIMP TOASTS WITH PICKLED CARROT

DISHES THAT CAN BE MADE AHEAD OF TIME ARE VERY USEFUL – ESPECIALLY IF YOU SERVE THESE WHEN ENTERTAINING! THE PRAWN MIXTURE HERE CAN BE 'PREPPED' SEVERAL HOURS IN ADVANCE AND THE TOASTS SIMPLY COOKED TO ORDER.

300 g/10 oz. uncooked prawns/shrimp, shelled and deveined

6 spring onions/scallions, thinly sliced on a diagonal

1 tablespoon fresh ginger, peeled and grated

2 teaspoons dry sherry (optional)

1 teaspoon light soy sauce

1 egg white, lightly beaten

6 thick slices of white bread

50 g/⅓ cup sesame seeds

about 250 ml/1 cup vegetable oil, for shallow-frying

sprigs of fresh coriander/cilantro, to garnish

salt, to season

FOR THE PICKLED CARROT

1 large carrot, coarsely grated

2 tablespoons Japanese pickled ginger, sliced

2 tablespoons juice from the pickled ginger jar

½ teaspoon caster/granulated sugar

2 shallots, thinly sliced on a diagonal

MAKES 24

To make the pickled carrot, combine the carrot, pickled ginger, pickled ginger juice, sugar and shallots in a small, non-reactive bowl. Set aside until needed.

Put the prawns, spring onions, ginger, sherry, soy sauce, egg white and some salt in a food processor or blender. Process until roughly chopped.

Trim the crusts off the bread and discard or save for another use. Cut each slice into 4 triangles. Put the sesame seeds on a plate. Spread about 2 teaspoons of the prawn mixture onto each piece of bread, pressing down lightly. Press each triangle into the sesame seeds to lightly coat.

Put the oil in a shallow frying pan/skillet and heat over a medium/high heat. Add a piece of bread to test if the oil is ready – if the bread sizzles on contact, the oil is hot enough. Use a fish slice to carefully add the prawn toasts to the pan, prawn-side down, and cook for 1 minute. Turn over and cook for 1 minute more, until golden. Drain on paper towels. Spoon a little pickled carrot over the top of each toast and add a sprig of coriander. Serve immediately.

SALT & PEPPER SQUID

A BEST-EVER VERSION OF A CLASSIC, OFTEN REQUESTED IN DIM SUM
RESTAURANTS. HERE IS HOW TO COOK THIS FAVOURITE IN THE COMFORT
OF YOUR OWN HOME.

3 fresh whole squid, cleaned

1 tablespoon Shaoxing rice wine

2 tablespoons sesame oil

vegetable oil, for deep-frying

100 g/¾ cup plain/all-purpose
   flour

50 g/⅓ cup semolina

1 teaspoon salt

1 tablespoon freshly ground
   white pepper

1 tablespoon sunflower/
   safflower oil

2 teaspoons fresh ginger,
   peeled and grated

2 garlic cloves, minced

2 small green chillies/chiles,
   deseeded and sliced

2 small red chillies/chiles,
   deseeded and sliced

2 curry leaves

salt and freshly ground black
   pepper, to season

SERVES 4–5 AS A SMALL DISH

Remove the tentacles from the body of the cleaned squid.
Slice the body widthways into 3-cm/1¼-in. thick strips. Cut
the tentacles into 4-cm/1½-in. long pieces. Place the squid
in a bowl with the Shaoxing rice wine and sesame oil. Cover with
clingfilm/plastic wrap and leave in the fridge to marinate
for 30 minutes.

Heat the oil in a deep-fryer or large pan until it reaches
180°C/350°F.

Mix together the flour, semolina, salt and white pepper
in a bowl. Toss the squid in the dry mixture to coat thoroughly.

Using a long-handled sieve/strainer, lower the squid into the
hot oil. Deep-fry until golden brown. Drain the cooked squid
on paper towels and season to taste with salt and pepper.

Add 1 tablespoon of oil to a wok over a medium heat and fry the
ginger for 1 minute until fragrant. Next add the garlic, chillies
and curry leaves. Fry for another 30 seconds until the garlic
is golden. Add the squid to the wok and stir-fry quickly for about
10 seconds. Serve immediately.

THAI FISHCAKES

NO POTATOES OR EGG ARE USED IN THESE FISHCAKES AND THE RESULTING
TOUGH-BUT-TASTY SKIN FORMED UPON COOKING IS DELICIOUS.

3 garlic cloves, peeled

1 red chilli/chile

2 onions, chopped

1 teaspoon chilli/chile powder

½ teaspoon ground cumin

½ teaspoon ground coriander

50 g/5 tablespoons fresh ginger, peeled and grated

1 teaspoon tamarind paste

grated zest and freshly squeezed juice of 1 lime

2 tablespoons fish sauce

400 g/14 oz. white fish fillet (such as hake, pollock, whiting or cod), chopped into 2-cm/¾-in. pieces

vegetable oil, for frying

FOR THE DIPPING SAUCE

2 tablespoons brown sugar

1 tablespoon dark soy sauce

2 tablespoons sesame oil

1 tablespoon fish sauce

freshly squeezed juice of 1 lime

½ carrot, finely diced

½ cucumber, finely diced

SERVES 4

Begin by making the dipping sauce. Heat the sugar, soy sauce, sesame oil and fish sauce in a saucepan set over a medium heat. Remove from the heat and let cool, before adding the lime juice, carrot and cucumber. Set aside until ready to serve.

Put the garlic, chilli and onions in a food processor or blender and pulse until finely chopped and combined. Add the spices, ginger, tamarind, lime zest and juice and fish sauce, and pulse again to combine. Finally, add the fish pieces and pulse briefly until fully combined – it should be the texture of a thick porridge. Don't over-blend the mixture once the fish has been added as it can easily become a paste.

Heat a little vegetable oil in a saucepan set over a medium heat. Scoop tablespoonfuls of the mixture into the hot pan. After about a minute, flip the fishcakes over and cook for a further minute, until golden brown. Serve warm with the dipping sauce.

PRAWNS/SHRIMP WRAPPED IN NOODLES WITH CHILLI/CHILE & GARLIC SAUCE

THESE MAKE A LOVELY CANAPÉS OR FINGER FOOD.

100 g/3½ oz. dried thin egg noodles

24 large uncooked prawns/ shrimp, shelled and deveined

vegetable oil, for deep-frying

Sweet Chilli/Chile Sauce (page 16), to serve

a baking sheet lined with baking parchment

SERVES 4

Put the noodles in a bowl, cover with boiling water and soak for 20 minutes until softened. Drain the noodles and pat dry with paper towels. Wrap 8–10 noodles around each prawn and set aside.

Preheat the oven to 110°C (225°F) Gas ¼ (or the lowest heat setting).

Pour vegetable oil into a wok or large saucepan to reach about 5 cm/2 in. up the side and set over a medium–high heat. Heat until a cube of bread dropped into the oil crisps in 30 seconds. Deep-fry the wrapped prawns in batches for 2–3 minutes until the noodles are crisp and prawns are cooked through.

Turn off the oven and set in the still-warm oven while you cook the remaining prawns in the same way.

Serve with the sweet chilli sauce.

FIERY BEEF SATAY
IN PEANUT SAUCE

BEEF, PORK OR CHICKEN SATAYS COOKED IN, OR SERVED WITH, A FIERY PEANUT SAUCE ARE HUGELY POPULAR THROUGHOUT SOUTHEAST ASIA. THIS PARTICULAR SAUCE IS A GREAT FAVOURITE IN THAILAND, VIETNAM AND INDONESIA. IT IS BEST TO MAKE YOUR OWN BUT COMMERCIAL BRANDS ARE AVAILABLE UNDER THE BANNER SATAY OR SATE SAUCE.

FOR THE SATAY

500 g/1 lb. beef sirloin, sliced against the grain into bite-sized pieces

1 tablespoon groundnut/peanut oil

FOR THE PEANUT SAUCE

60 ml/¼ cup peanut or vegetable oil

4–5 garlic cloves, minced

4–5 dried serrano chillies/chiles, deseeded and ground with a pestle and mortar

1–2 teaspoons curry powder

60 g/½ cup roasted peanuts, finely ground

TO SERVE

a small bunch of fresh coriander/cilantro

a small bunch of fresh mint

lime wedges

a packet of short wooden or bamboo skewers, soaked in water before use

SERVES 4–6

To make the sauce, heat the oil in a heavy-based saucepan and stir in the garlic until it begins to colour. Add the chillies, curry powder and the peanuts and stir over a gentle heat, until the mixture forms a paste. Remove from the heat and leave to cool.

Put the beef pieces in a bowl. Beat the oil into the sauce and tip the mixture onto the beef. Mix together well, so that the beef is evenly coated and thread the meat onto the prepared skewers.

Prepare a charcoal or conventional grill. Cook the satays for 2–3 minutes on each side, then serve the skewered meat with the fresh herbs to wrap around each tasty morsel, and lime wedges for squeezing.

ASIAN CARAMEL WINGS

A RICH, BITTERSWEET SAUCE THAT ADDS AN ASIAN FEEL TO CHICKEN WINGS. FRIED AND TOSSED IN THE MARINADE, THESE WINGS HAVE THE PERFECT BALANCE OF DELICATE SEASONING. SERVE ALONGSIDE THE GREEN ONION DIPPING SAUCE, WITH EGG-FRIED RICE, IF LIKED.

200 g/1 cup brown sugar

75 ml/⅓ cup fish sauce

75 ml/⅓ cup soy sauce

60 ml/¼ cup orange juice

60 ml/¼ cup freshly squeezed lime juice

1.8 kg/4 lbs. chicken wings, halved at the joints, tips removed

vegetable oil, for frying

Egg Fried Rice (Page 70), to serve (optional)

FOR THE GREEN ONION DIPPING SAUCE

250 ml/1 cup sour cream

225 g/1 cup mayonnaise

50 g/½ cup spring onions/ scallions, thinly sliced on a diagonal

30 g/½ cup finely chopped fresh flat-leaf parsley

2 garlic cloves, minced

1 teaspoon Dijon mustard

SERVES 4–6

For the dipping sauce, mix all the ingredients together in a blender until smooth.

Refrigerate until ready to serve. Place the sugar in a medium saucepan with 60 ml/¼ cup water and set over a medium-high heat to bring to the boil. Continue to boil and swirl (don't stir) for 6–7 minutes so the sugar caramelizes evenly.

Combine the fish sauce, soy sauce, orange juice and lime juice with 60 ml/¼ cup water in a cup.

Once the caramel has turned a golden amber colour, slowly pour in the mixture and return to the boil. Continue to boil for 7 minutes until the sauce is well combined, then remove from the heat and keep warm.

Meanwhile, preheat the oil in a deep fryer to 180°C (350°F).

Fry the chicken wings in batches for about 10 minutes until cooked through and the juices run clear when the thickest part is pierced to the bone. Remove and drain on paper towels. Place in a large bowl, pour the caramel sauce over the wings and toss.

Serve with the dipping sauce and egg-fried rice on the side, if liked.

CHAPTER

✳

3

CHICKEN NOODLE SOUP

IT'S NO WONDER CHICKEN SOUP IS KNOWN FOR ITS SOOTHING MEDICINAL
PROPERTIES AS WELL AS ITS FLAVOUR – IT TASTES SO GOOD AND SO HEALTHY
WITH AN UNDERLYING HINT OF GINGER AND GARLIC FROM THE STOCK. A SIMPLE
SOUP, BUT WITH A REALLY GOOD STOCK AS A BASE IT'S HARD TO BEAT.

200 g/7 oz. dried Hokkien
    noodles

1.25 litres/2 quarts
    chicken stock

2 teaspoons fresh ginger,
    peeled and grated

2 tablespoons light soy sauce

2 tablespoons shaoxing
    rice wine

1 tablespoon oyster sauce

200 g/1½ cups sliced chicken
    breast fillet

250 g/about 6 whole pak choi/
    bok choy, trimmed and
    roughly chopped

2 spring onions/scallions,
    thinly sliced on a diagonal,
    plus extra to serve

salt, to season

fresh chillies/chiles, deseeded
    and sliced, to garnish
    (optional)

a small bunch of fresh
    coriander/cilantro, to garnish
    (optional)

SERVES 4

Plunge the noodles into a saucepan of boiling water and cook
for 3–4 minutes until al dente. Drain, refresh under cold water
and shake dry. Set aside.

Pour the stock into a large saucepan with the ginger, soy sauce,
rice wine and oyster sauce and set over a medium heat. Bring
slowly to the boil, then simmer for 5 minutes.

Stir in the chicken, pak choi and spring onions and simmer
for 3–4 minutes until the chicken is cooked.

Divide the noodles between bowls, pour over the chicken soup
and serve with some sliced chillies and fresh coriander, if using.

Tip: If using fresh Hokkien noodles cook for 2 minutes instead
of 3–4. If using vacuum-packed, pre-cooked noodles rinse under
boiling water only before use. For either you will need 500 g/1 lb.

GINGER COCONUT BROTH
WITH VEGGIES & NOODLES

THIS FALLS SOMEWHERE BETWEEN A SOUP, A CURRY AND A BROTHY RAMEN BOWL. WITH GINGER, CHILLI AND GARLIC FLAVOURS IT OFTEN HITS THE SPOT WHEN LOOKING FOR SOMETHING THAT YOU CAN SLURP A BIG BOWL OF WITHOUT IT WEIGHING YOU DOWN.

FOR THE BROTH

2 teaspoons avocado oil

4 garlic cloves, minced

2 tablespoons fresh ginger, peeled and grated

1 x 400-ml/14-oz. can coconut milk

2 tablespoons tamari

120 ml/½ cup water or vegetable stock/broth

¼ teaspoon chilli flakes/hot red pepper flakes (optional)

ADD-INS

120-170 g/4-6 oz. soba noodles

1 courgette/zucchini, peeled or spiralized into noodles or cut into julienne

1 carrot, spiralized into noodles or cut into julienne

130 g/1 cup shelled frozen edamame beans, thawed

SERVES 2–3

Cook the soba noodles in boiling water according to the package instructions.

While the soba noodles are cooking, heat the avocado oil in a large saucepan or high-sided frying pan/skillet over a medium-high heat. Add the garlic and ginger and let them sizzle for about 30–60 seconds until fragrant, but not browning.

Add the coconut milk and tamari and stir. Add the water or vegetable stock and chilli flakes (if using). Bring to a simmer, then stir in the courgette, carrot and edamame beans and let everything warm through for about 2 minutes. Remove from the heat.

Divide the cooked soba noodles between bowls and pour the hot broth and veggies over to serve.

GREEN THAI SOUP

THIS SOUP IS PERFECT FOR USING UP ALL YOUR GREEN VEG. IT HAS THAI
SPICES FROM GREEN CURRY PASTE, CREAMINESS FROM COCONUT MILK, AND
IT'S PACKED TO THE BRIM WITH VEGETABLES. YOU CAN USE SPINACH (FRESH
OR FROZEN) OR SWISS CHARD IN PLACE OF KALE, OR THROW IN THAT RANDOM
KOHLRABI THAT YOU DON'T KNOW WHAT TO DO WITH – IT'S ALL GOOD IN THIS
SOUP. YOU CAN SERVE THIS MOSTLY PURÉED, WITH A HELPING OF BROWN
RICE FOR TEXTURE AND BULK; BUT YOU CAN SKIP THE BLENDER AND KEEP
IT CHUNKY IF YOU PREFER.

vegetable oil, for frying

1 leek, thinly sliced on a
diagonal, white and light
green parts only,

salt, to season

2 garlic cloves, minced

2 tablespoons Green Curry
Paste (page 10)

1 broccoli crown with stems,
chopped into small pieces

475 ml/2 cups boiling water

1 courgette/zucchini, roughly
chopped

125 g/1 cup frozen peas

2 large handfuls of kale, stems
removed and roughly chopped

1 x 400-ml/14-oz. can coconut
milk

5 sprigs of freshly chopped
coriander/cilantro with stems

cooked brown rice, to serve
(optional)

SERVES 3–4

In a large saucepan with a lid, heat a good glug of oil over
a medium-high heat. Add the leek, season to taste with salt and
cook, stirring occasionally, for about 5–7 minutes, until the leek
has softened.

Add the garlic and fry for another minute. Stir in the curry paste
and cook for another minute. Add the broccoli and boiling water
to the pan and stir. Bring to a simmer and add the courgette.
Cover the pan and simmer for about 5 minutes until the
vegetables are tender.

Stir in the peas and kale, cover, and cook for another
1–2 minutes until the kale has wilted. Turn off the heat and
stir in coconut milk (reserving a little to garnish) and coriander.

If blending, use a stick blender or purée in batches in a food
processor or blender until mostly smooth.

Serve the soup in bowls with extra coriander, a drizzle of the
reserved coconut milk and a portion of cooked brown rice,
if desired.

HOT & SOUR SOUP WITH PRAWNS/SHRIMP (TOM YAM KUNG)

ALTHOUGH WESTERNERS LIKE TO HAVE SOUP AS A SEPARATE COURSE, IN THAILAND IT IS SERVED WITH OTHER DISHES. PEOPLE LADLE SPOONFULS OF SOUP FROM A COMMUNAL BOWL ONTO THE RICE ON THEIR PLATES.

1.25 litres/5 quarts chicken stock

1 tablespoon tom yam sauce

4 makrut lime leaves, finely chopped

2 lemongrass stalks, thickly sliced

3 tablespoons freshly squeezed lemon or lime juice

3 tablespoons Thai fish sauce

2 small fresh red or green chillies/chiles, deseeded and sliced

2 teaspoons caster/granulated sugar

12 straw mushrooms, halved (canned mushrooms will do)

12 uncooked king prawns/jumbo shrimp, shelled and deveined

SERVES 4

Heat the stock in a saucepan and add the tom yam sauce. Add the lime leaves, lemongrass, lemon juice, fish sauce, chillies and sugar. Bring to the boil and simmer for 2 minutes.

Add the mushrooms and prawns, stir and cook for a further 2–3 minutes, or until the prawns are cooked through. Ladle into soup bowls and serve.

Note: Tom yam sauce is widely available, even in some supermarkets. If you can't find it, try an Oriental market or online.

SUNSHINE LAKSA WITH CRAB & MANGETOUTS/SNOW PEAS

SO BRIGHT, SO SUNNY AND SO DELICATE! THIS RECIPE IS A GREAT ILLUSTRATION OF SUBTLE UMAMI FLAVOURS, RATHER THAN THE PUNCHY TOMATO, HAM AND CHEESE RECIPES THAT COMMONLY FEATURE WHEN CAPTURING SAVOURY DELICIOUSNESS. YOU CAN REPLACE THE MILLET WITH BROWN RICE OR ANY WHOLEGRAIN OF YOUR CHOICE.

200 g/1 cup millet

1 tablespoon vegetable oil

2 x 400-ml/14-oz. cans coconut milk

500 ml/2 cups chicken stock

2 tablespoons fish sauce

5 makrut lime leaves

1 lemongrass stalk, crushed

freshly squeezed juice of 3 limes

250 g/9 oz. white crab meat

200 g/3 small handfuls mangetouts/snow peas, cut on a diagonal into 1-cm/½-in. pieces

4 spring onions/scallions, thinly sliced on a diagonal

TO SERVE

2 red chillies/chiles, deseeded and sliced

1 handful of freshly chopped coriander/cilantro

lime wedges

FOR THE LAKSA PASTE

3 shallots, cut in half

3 garlic cloves

3 red chillies/chiles, (1 with the seeds left in and 2 deseeded; leave more with seeds in if you want it hotter)

2 lemongrass stalks, chopped

2.5-cm/1-in. square piece of fresh ginger, coarsely chopped

1½ tablespoons any nut or seed butter

2 teaspoons shrimp paste

2 teaspoons curry powder

½ teaspoon salt

1 tablespoon vegetable oil

SERVES 4

Place all the laksa paste ingredients in a small food processor or blender and blitz to a paste.

Cook the millet according to the packet instructions, set aside and leave covered to stay warm.

Heat the oil in a large heavy-based saucepan over a high heat. Add the laksa paste and cook for 1 minute to release all the aromatics. Add the coconut milk, chicken stock, 500 ml/2 cups water, fish sauce, makrut lime leaves and lemongrass to the pot and bring to the boil for 10 minutes. Remove from the heat and add the lime juice.

Take some warm serving bowls and in the base put 1½ tablespoons of millet, 1½ tablespoons crab meat, one-quarter of the mangetouts and some spring onions. Ladle over the piping hot broth. Serve with the red chillies, coriander and lime wedges.

SWEET POTATO & MISO SOUP
WITH SEAWEED

SWEET POTATO AND MISO PASTE IS A PERFECT MARRIAGE; IT'S ONE OF THOSE
UNIDENTIFIABLE FLAVOUR COMBINATIONS THAT KEEPS PEOPLE COMING BACK.
THIS SOUP IS RICH WITH SALTY, SAVOURY AND SWEET ELEMENTS COMBINING
TO GIVE A REMARKABLE DEPTH OF FLAVOUR.

20 g/1 cup dried mixed seaweed

**70 g/4½ tablespoons yellow
miso paste**

**4 sweet potatoes, peeled and
roughly diced**

**100 ml/scant ½ cup double/
heavy cream**

salt, to season

SERVES 4

Put the seaweed in a large mixing bowl and cover with boiling
water. Add 20 g/1¼ tablespoons of the miso paste and a pinch
of table salt. Stir, then leave for 20 minutes for the seaweed
to rehydrate.

Put the sweet potatoes into a saucepan with the remaining miso
paste and just cover with cold water. Cover and bring to a low
simmer over a medium heat. Simmer for 15 minutes. Check the
sweet potatoes with a knife – they should be soft and cooked
through. Simmer for another 5 minutes if needed.

Remove the pan from the heat and, using a stick blender, purée
the miso broth and sweet potato to a smooth consistency.
Add the cream and a pinch of salt, and blend to combine.

Drain the rehydrated seaweed. Pour the soup into bowls and
decorate with the seaweed to serve.

SPICY PUMPKIN & COCONUT SOUP WITH GINGER & LIME

THIS BEAUTIFUL ORANGE AND GREEN SOUP WITH ITS SWEET-SOUR FLAVOUR AND HINT OF CHILLI/CHILE HEAT MAKES AN EXOTIC START TO A SPECIAL MEAL. DESPITE THE RICHNESS OF THE COCONUT MILK, THE SHARPNESS OF THE LIME KEEPS IT TASTING LIGHT. YOU CAN USE ANY ORANGE-FLESHED WINTER SQUASH OR COOKING PUMPKIN FOR THIS RECIPE.

2 tablespoons sunflower/safflower oil

750 g/1½ lbs pumpkin or butternut squash, peeled, deseeded and cut into 2-cm/¾-in. chunks

a bunch of spring onions/scallions, thinly sliced on a diagonal

5-cm/2-in. piece of fresh ginger, coarsely chopped

2 garlic cloves, minced

2–3 red chillies/chiles, deseeded and sliced, plus extra slices to garnish

2 lemongrass stalks, spilt lengthways

a large bunch of fresh coriander/cilantro, stalks and leaves separated

1.2 litres/5 quarts vegetable or chicken stock

1 x 400-ml/14-oz. can coconut milk

2–3 tablespoons Thai fish sauce

freshly squeezed juice of 1–2 limes

crème fraîche/sour cream, to serve

SERVES 6

Heat the oil in a large saucepan and, over a low heat, sweat the pumpkin and spring onions with a pinch of salt until soft but not browned, about 15–20 minutes.

Meanwhile, put the ginger, garlic, chillies, lemongrass and coriander stalks in another saucepan with the stock and simmer gently, covered, for 20–25 minutes.

Let the stock cool slightly, then liquidize and sieve/strain into the saucepan with the pumpkin mixture, pressing hard on the contents of the sieve/strainer to extract maximum flavour. Discard the debris in the sieve, then process or liquidize the liquid again with the pumpkin mixture until smooth.

Return the soup to the rinsed-out saucepan, add the coconut milk, 2 tablespoons fish sauce and the juice of 1 lime, then reheat, stirring all the time, to just below boiling point. Adjust the seasoning, adding more fish sauce and lime juice to taste. Chop most of the coriander leaves finely and stir into the soup (keep a few roughly chopped leaves to scatter over the soup at the end). Heat for a few minutes, but do not allow to boil.

Serve piping hot, topped with a spoonful of crème fraîche and scattered with the reserved chopped coriander leaves and/or some extra red chilli slices.

SLOW ROAST BELLY PORK, NOODLES & SHIITAKE MUSHROOMS IN SOUR BROTH

a 400-g/14-oz. piece of belly pork

2 tablespoons vegetable oil

½ red onion, finely sliced

2.5-cm/1-in. piece of fresh ginger, peeled and grated

150 g/5½ oz. shiitake or mixed exotic Chinese mushrooms

250 g/1 cup canned beef consommé

1.5 litres/6¼ quarts chicken stock

200 g/7 oz. soba or other buckwheat noodles

2–3 green chillies/chiles, deseeded and sliced

4 spring onions/scallions, thinly sliced on a diagonal, whites and greens separated

2 teaspoons sesame oil

2 tablespoons mirin (Japanese rice wine)

2 tablespoons soy sauce, plus extra to taste

3–4 tablespoons rice vinegar, plus extra to taste

150 g/5½ oz. canned water chestnuts, drained and sliced

2 heads of pak choi/bok choy

a roasting pan, lightly oiled

SERVES 6–8

THIS IS ONE OF THOSE SOUPS THAT YOU KNOW WILL TASTE GOOD BECAUSE IT LOOKS A BIT INTRIGUING: A CLEAR BROTH OF GREAT FLAVOURS AND TEXTURES. THE CRUNCH OF THE WATER CHESTNUTS IS A LOVELY CONTRAST TO THE SLIPPERY NATURE OF THE MUSHROOMS. THE MIXTURE OF RICH, SWEET, SALTY AND SOUR IS TYPICAL OF CHINESE FOOD, AND THIS SOUP DEMONSTRATES ALL THESE CHARACTERISTICS BRILLIANTLY.

Preheat the oven to 220°C (425°F) Gas 7.

Put the pork belly in the prepared roasting pan and roast for 30 minutes, then turn the temperature down to 180°C (350°F) Gas 4 and roast for a further 30 minutes. Pour off any fat, remove the crackling (and reserve for the garnish) and cut the meat into even slices. Set aside.

Heat the oil in a large saucepan, add the onion and ginger and toss over a medium heat until softened. Add the mushrooms to the pan and stir to coat with the oil. Pour in the consommé and stock and bring the liquid to a simmer. Add the noodles, chillies, spring onion whites and pork slices, and simmer for 5–7 minutes, until the noodles are tender.

Add the sesame oil, mirin, soy sauce, rice vinegar and water chestnuts. Adjust the seasoning by adding more soy sauce and vinegar. When happy with the balance of sweet, salt and sour, add the spring onion greens and the pak choi and cook for a further 2 minutes.

Serve in Chinese bowls, garnished with pieces of crackling.

PEPPERED BEEF PHO

THE BEST THING ABOUT PHO IS ALL THE SAUCES AND HERBS THAT GO ALONG
WITH IT. YOU CAN MAKE A SIMPLE BOWL OR GO TO TOWN AND REALLY DRESS
IT UP – THERE ARE NO RULES!

1.5 litres/6 cups good-quality chicken stock

2 star anise

2.5-cm/1-in. piece of fresh ginger

2 tablespoons fish sauce

2 tablespoons toasted sesame oil

3 tablespoons soy sauce

1 tablespoon sambal oelek (Asian chilli/chile paste)

1 teaspoon Lampong peppercorns, cracked

1 garlic clove, minced

450 g/1 lb. sirloin steak

600 g/4 cups cooked rice noodles

115 g/2 cups beansprouts

135 g/1 cup grated carrot

3 spring onions/scallions, thinly sliced on a diagonal

2 red chillies/chiles, deseeded and sliced

selection of fresh Vietnamese basil, mint, coriander/cilantro, lime wedges and chilli/chile sauce, to serve

SERVES 4

Pour the chicken stock into a saucepan and add the star anise, ginger and fish sauce. Bring to the boil, then reduce the heat and simmer for 20 minutes.

In a shallow bowl, whisk together the sesame oil, soy sauce, sambal oelek, peppercorns and garlic. Add the steak and coat with the marinade.

Set a heavy-based cast-iron frying pan/skillet over a high heat until smoking. Add the steak and sear for 2 minutes on each side, then transfer to a cutting board. Reduce the heat and add the remainder of the marinade to the pan. Cook for a few minutes until thickened, then pour into a small bowl.

Remove the ginger and star anise from the broth. Slice the steak into thin strips. Divide the noodles, beansprouts and grated carrot into four large bowls. Top with strips of steak and pour over the hot broth. Sprinkle with the spring onions and chillies. Serve with the fresh herbs, lime wedges and sauce.

NOODLES & RICE

VEGETARIAN EGG NOODLES

MAKING NOODLES FROM SCRATCH IS REWARDING AND ACTUALLY RELATIVELY EASY. ADD MARINATED TOFU TO BULK OUT IF DESIRED.

1 tablespoon groundnut/peanut oil

1 garlic clove, minced

1 teaspoon fresh ginger, peeled and grated

1 large red (bell) pepper, chopped

1 carrot, peeled and thinly sliced

stir-fry sauce of choice

60 g/1 cup beansprouts

2 heads of pak choi/bok choy, sliced

1 red chilli/chile, deseeded and sliced, plus extra to serve

freshly chopped coriander/cilantro, to serve

spring onion/scallion, thinly sliced on a diagonal, to serve

FOR THE EGG DOUGH

150 g/1 cup plus 2 tablespoons Asian white wheat flour

1 egg

SERVES 4

For the noodles, put the flour in a large mixing bowl and add 3 tablespoons water and the egg. Bring together, then turn the dough out onto a lightly floured surface. Using lightly floured hands, knead for 20–25 minutes. The dough will be sticky at first but should become smooth and silky. Cover with a damp kitchen cloth to prevent from drying out and set aside to rest in the fridge for 30 minutes.

To make the noodles, lightly dust the countertop with flour and roll out the dough into one big thin rectangle. Using a sharp knife, cut the dough into 1 cm/½ in. thin strips. Lightly dust the noodles with a little more flour to prevent them from sticking together.

Cook the noodles in a pan of boiling water until tender, around 3 minutes. Drain and cool the noodles in ice-cold water to rinse off the starch. Set aside while you prepare the vegetables.

Heat the groundnut oil in a wok and gently cook the garlic and ginger until fragrant. Add the (bell) pepper and carrot and lightly fry for a further few minutes before adding the noodles. Flavour the noodles with the stir-fry sauce. Lastly, add the beansprouts, pak choi and chilli.

Serve the dish straight away with the coriander, spring onion and chilli and extra stir-fry sauce to taste.

EGG FRIED RICE

A CLASSIC AND SIMPLE DISH – YOU CAN ALSO TREAT THIS AS A WAY TO USE UP
LEFTOVER VEG, BUT THIS RECIPE JUST USES FROZEN PEAS.

2 tablespoons groundnut/
   peanut or vegetable oil

2 garlic cloves, minced

100 g/¾ cup frozen peas

550 g/4 cups cold, cooked
   jasmine rice

3 eggs, lightly beaten

2 tablespoons light soy sauce,
   plus extra if needed

2 teaspoons toasted sesame oil

salt and freshly ground black
   pepper, to season

SERVES 4

Heat the oil in a wok or large frying pan/skillet until very hot,
then add the garlic and stir-fry over a high heat for 1 minute.
Throw in the peas and cook for a further minute.

Add the rice to the wok and stir, breaking up any lumps.

Season the beaten eggs with a pinch of salt and black pepper.
Make a well in the centre of the wok and pour in the eggs.
When the bottom starts to set, scramble the eggs with a wooden
spoon until softly set in light, fluffy curds, then stir through the
rice. Stir in the soy sauce and sesame oil. Taste and add a little
more soy sauce or salt if you think it needs it.

CRISPY RICE WITH SOY & GINGER TEMPEH

AT FIRST GLANCE, SOY-RICE-SPECKLED TEMPEH SEEMS NEITHER ATTRACTIVE NOR INSPIRING – BUT ITS SAVING GRACE IS THAT IT DOES ABSORB STRONG FLAVOURS AND MARINADES VERY WELL. IT RESPONDS WELL TO BAKING TOO, SO THIS IS ONE OF THOSE DISHES THAT DIE HARD MEAT-EATERS ARE REALLY VERY PLEASANTLY SURPRISED BY.

200 g/7 oz. tempeh

5 tablespoons dark soy sauce

1 tablespoon sesame oil

1 teaspoon caster/granulated sugar

30 g/1 oz. fresh ginger, peeled and grated

2 garlic cloves, minced

200 g/generous 1 cup basmati rice

3 tablespoon olive oil

a bunch of spring onions/ scallions, thinly sliced on a diagonal

a bunch of freshly chopped coriander/cilantro

1 tablespoon white sesame seeds, to garnish

a deep baking pan, lined with baking parchment

SERVES 4

Preheat the oven to 190°C (375°F) Gas 5.

Cut the tempeh into slices. Mix the soy sauce, sesame oil and sugar together in a large bowl. Stir in the grated ginger and garlic. Toss the tempeh slices in the mixture and leave to marinate.

Rinse the rice under running water, until the water runs clear. Scatter it over the base of the lined baking pan. Pour in 800 ml/ scant 3½ cups water and bake for about 30 minutes, until the water has been absorbed and the rice is cooked. Remove the pan from the oven and drizzle over the olive oil.

Remove the tempeh from the marinade and lay it in a row down the centre of the rice. Return to the oven and bake for about 10 minutes, until the tempeh is hot and the rice is crisp.

Scatter over the spring onions, coriander and sesame seeds, and serve.

SINGAPORE NOODLES

2 teaspoons curry powder

300 g/2½ cups fresh egg noodles

2 tablespoons sunflower/safflower oil

300 g/4½ cups (about 30) uncooked prawns/shrimp, shelled and deveined

75 g/3 oz. char sui, sliced

a bunch of spring onions/scallions, thinly sliced on a diagonal

1 red (bell) pepper, thinly sliced

2 eggs, beaten

2 tablespoons groundnut/peanut oil

2 garlic cloves, sliced

2.5-cm/1-in. piece of fresh ginger, peeled and grated

100 g/1¾ cups beansprouts, trimmed

6 garlic chives, snipped

garlic chive flowers, to garnish (optional)

sambal olek (Asian chilli/chile paste), to serve

FOR THE SAUCE

2 tablespoons light soy sauce

1 tablespoon caster/granulated sugar

1 teaspoon sesame oil

2 tablespoons oyster sauce

2 tablespoons rice wine vinegar

SERVES 4

THIS DELICIOUS NOODLE DISH IS BOTH REFRESHING AND COMFORTING, PACKED WITH PRAWNS/SHRIMP, VEGETABLES AND THE AUTHENTIC FLAVOURS OF SINGAPORE.

Begin by making the sauce. Combine all the ingredients in a small mixing bowl and set aside.

Next combine the curry powder with 2 teaspoons water to make a paste. Set aside.

Cook the noodles by plunging them into a large saucepan of boiling water. Return to the boil and cook for 1 minute until al dente. Drain well and rinse under cold water to remove any excess starch. Set aside.

Put the sunflower oil in a wok or large frying pan/skillet set over a high heat and warm until smoking. Add the prawns and stir-fry for 2–3 minutes until lightly golden. Remove with a slotted spoon and set aside.

Fry the char sui in the same pan for 1 minute, remove and set aside. Cook the spring onions and pepper for 2 minutes, remove from pan and set aside.

Reduce the heat, add the beaten egg and cook in a single layer for 2 minutes. Remove from the pan, roll up and allow to cool before cutting into thin strips.

Add the groundnut/peanut oil to the wok and stir-fry the garlic and ginger for 1 minute, then stir in the reserved curry paste. Add the noodles to the pan with the reserved sauce and toss over a high heat for 2 minutes until heated through.

Stir through the prawns, char sui, spring onions, peppers, egg strips, beansprouts and chives for 1–2 minutes until hot.

Serve in bowls garnished with chive flowers, if using, and some sambal olek.

BEEF CHOW MEIN

300 g/10½ oz. sirloin beef or fillet, trimmed of fat and very thinly sliced

300 g/10½ oz. fresh medium egg noodles

1½ tablespoons groundnut/peanut oil

3 spring onions/scallions, thinly sliced on a diagonal, white and green parts separated

170 g/6 oz. choy sum (or pak-choi/bok choy), chopped into 2-cm/¾-in. pieces, stalks and leaves separated

1 red chilli/chile, deseeded and sliced, to garnish (optional)

FOR THE MARINADE

1½ tablespoons dark soy sauce

½ tablespoon Chinese rice wine

½ teaspoon caster/granulated sugar

1 garlic clove, minced

1 teaspoon fresh ginger, peeled and grated

2 teaspoons cornflour/cornstarch

FOR THE SAUCE

2 tablespoons oyster sauce

200 ml/¾ cup chicken stock

1 tablespoon light soy sauce

1 tablespoon dark soy sauce

2 teaspoons cornflour/cornstarch

SERVES 2

CHOW MEIN IS A CLASSIC NOODLE STIR-FRY THAT SHOULD BE PART OF EVERY KEEN COOK'S REPERTOIRE. TREAT THIS RECIPE AS A BASIC GUIDE TO WHICH YOU CAN ADD YOUR OWN TOUCHES. TRY VARYING THE VEGETABLES AND REPLACING THE BEEF WITH CHICKEN OR EVEN TOFU.

Put the beef in a bowl, add all the marinade ingredients, mix well and set aside.

Bring a saucepan of water to the boil. Throw in the noodles and blanch for 2–3 minutes. Drain and rinse under cold running water. Set aside.

Combine all the sauce ingredients in a bowl and set aside.

Heat 1 tablespoon of the oil in a wok or large frying pan/skillet until hot. Add the marinated beef in two batches and stir-fry over a high heat for 2–3 minutes, or until well sealed all over. Remove the beef from the wok and set aside.

Heat the remaining oil in the wok, then add the white parts of the spring onions and stir-fry for just 30 seconds. Add the stalks of the choy sum and stir-fry for 2 minutes. Pour in the sauce and bring to the boil. Leave to bubble for 1 minute, then return the beef to the wok and stir through.

Stir the drained noodles into the wok, then cook a medium heat for 1–2 minutes, or until the noodles are tender. Divide the chow mein between two bowls, garnish with the remaining spring onions and the chilli, if using, and serve immediately.

CHICKEN PAD THAI

SPICY AND SATISFYING, THIS STREET FOOD FAVOURITE PACKS IN ALL THE FLAVOURS OF THAILAND. THE SHRIMP PASTE ADDS A DISTINCTIVE SAVOURY DEPTH TO THE DISH, SO DON'T LET ITS PUNGENT AROMA PUT YOU OFF. AND DON'T FORGET THE SQUEEZE OF LIME AT THE END.

150 g/5½ oz. dried flat Thai rice noodles

2 large garlic cloves, minced

1 large red chilli/chile, deseeded and sliced, plus ½, deseeded and sliced, to garnish

1 teaspoon shrimp paste (optional)

1 tablespoon vegetable oil, plus extra if needed

2 skinless chicken breasts, cut into 2-cm/¾-in. pieces

2 tablespoons fish sauce

2 eggs, lightly beaten

100 g/1 cup beansprouts

40 g/small bunch Chinese chives, cut into 4-cm/1½-in. lengths

1 tablespoon tamarind paste

1 tablespoon soft light brown sugar

3 tablespoons chopped roasted peanuts

2 spring onions/scallions, green and light green parts only, thinly sliced on the diagonal

a squeeze of fresh lime juice

2 tablespoons freshly chopped coriander/cilantro leaves, to garnish

lime wedges, to serve

SERVES 2

Put the noodles in a large heatproof bowl and cover with boiling water. Soak for 20 minutes, or until softened but not cooked through. Drain well.

Meanwhile, put the garlic, chilli and shrimp paste, if using, in a pestle and mortar and grind until you have a rough paste. Alternatively, blitz in a food processor or blender with a little water.

Heat the oil in a wok or large frying pan/skillet until very hot. Add the paste and fry over a high heat for 1 minute, or until fragrant. Season the chicken with ½ tablespoon of the fish sauce and add to the wok. Stir-fry for 4 minutes, or until just cooked through. Remove the chicken from the wok and set aside.

Heat another ½ tablespoon oil in the wok, if necessary. When hot, pour in the beaten eggs. Leave the bottom to set, then break up with a spoon to get softly set scrambled eggs. Return the chicken to the wok with the drained noodles, beansprouts and Chinese chives. Stir well.

Meanwhile, combine the remaining fish sauce with the tamarind paste and soft light brown sugar, then add to the wok with half the peanuts. Stir-fry for 2–4 minutes, or until the noodles are tender. You may need to sprinkle in a little water if the noodles look too dry. Stir in the spring onions and lime juice. Taste and add more fish sauce if you think it needs it.

Divide the pad Thai between two bowls, garnish with the chopped coriander, chilli and remaining peanuts and serve immediately with lime wedges.

STICKY RICE WITH CHINESE SAUSAGE

THIS IS GREAT TO TAKE ON JOURNEYS, AS ONCE COOKED, IT REMAINS MOIST
AND STICKY IN ITS TUPPERWARE OR BANANA LEAF AND CAN BE CONSUMED
HOT OR COLD.

vegetable oil, for frying

3 Asian shallots, chopped

1 spring onion/scallion, thinly sliced on a diagonal, plus extra, to serve

1 'lac xung' Chinese sausage (45g/1½ oz.), thinly sliced

15g/3 teaspoons dried shrimps, soaked in warm water for 10 mins, then drained and patted dry

10g/⅓ cup dried shiitake mushrooms, soaked in warm water for 20 mins, then drained and patted dry

400g/2 cups sticky/glutinous rice, soaked in warm water for 1 hour, then drained

a pinch of salt, to season

a pinch of freshly ground black pepper, to season

½ teaspoon sugar

a pinch of pork seasoning

Vietnamese pickles, to serve (optional)

Vietnamese ham, sliced, to serve (optional)

a steamer

SERVES 4

Heat the oil in a frying pan/skillet and fry the shallots and spring onion until softened, then add the sausage, shrimps and mushrooms and fry for 5 minutes. Add this to the rice in a large bowl with salt, pepper, sugar and seasoning and mix it together.

Bring the water in the steamer to a simmer. Place the rice mixture around the steamer, creating a hole for steam to flow in the middle. Steam for 30–40 minutes on medium heat, stirring the rice around every 10 minutes so that steam is flowing evenly and checking that there is enough water in the base. Take off the heat and leave to steam for another 10 minutes.

Serve hot with pickles, a sprinkle of spring onions and sliced Vietnamese ham. Alternatively, pack into banana leaf parcels which can be re-steamed when ready to serve.

CURRIES & STEWS

CHAPTER ☀ 5

RED CURRY WITH PRAWNS/SHRIMP & PUMPKIN

THAI CURRY IS A GREAT FLAVOUR HIT WHEN YOU GET IN FROM A BUSY DAY.
READY-MADE PASTES MAKE EVERYTHING EASIER BUT YOUR CURRY WILL
ONLY BE AS GOOD AS YOUR PASTE. LOOK FOR THAI BRANDS, WHICH ARE
GOOD BUT CAN OFTEN BE VERY HOT, OR MAKE YOUR OWN AND FREEZE
IT IN SMALL PORTIONS (PAGE 11).

1 x 400-ml/14-oz. can coconut milk

2 tablespoons Red Curry Paste (page 11, or store-bought)

2 tablespoons palm sugar/jaggery

1 lemongrass stalk, cut in half and bruised

400 g/14 oz. pumpkin or butternut squash, peeled, deseeded and cut into 2-cm/¾-in. chunks

125 g/4 oz. sugar snap peas, cut on a diagonal

200 g/7 oz. uncooked tiger prawns/shrimp, shelled, deveined and butterflied but tails intact

2 tablespoons Thai fish sauce

15 fresh mint leaves, finely shredded

1 large red chilli/chile, deseeded and sliced into thin strips

steamed jasmine rice, to serve

SERVES 4

If you remember, put the coconut milk in the fridge as soon as you buy it.

When you are ready to start cooking, scrape off the thick coconut cream which usually clings to the lid and put just the cream in a wok or large saucepan over a medium heat. Add the curry paste and stir for 1–2 minutes until the paste smells fragrant, then add the sugar and cook for a further 2 minutes until sticky.

Pour in the rest of the coconut milk, add the lemongrass, pumpkin and 100–120 ml/⅓–½ cup water to almost cover the pumpkin. Bring the contents of the wok to a gentle simmer and leave to bubble away gently for 10 minutes, or until the pumpkin is tender.

Add the sugar snap peas and cook for 2 minutes, then add the prawns and cook for a further 2 minutes, or until they turn pink.

Remove from the heat and stir in the fish sauce. Transfer to bowls and sprinkle with the mint and chilli. Taste and add more fish sauce if necessary. Serve with steamed jasmine rice.

CHICKEN KATSU CURRY & RICE

JAPANESE CURRY IS NOW A LUNCH FAVOURITE ALL AROUND THE WORLD. CURRY POWDER WAS FIRST SOLD IN CHINESE MEDICINE SHOPS IN JAPAN, AND 'KATSU' REFERS TO THE BREADED CUTLET ALSO INSPIRED BY WESTERN CUISINE.

FOR THE CURRY SAUCE

2 tablespoons vegetable oil

1 onion, finely chopped

1 carrot, peeled and finely chopped

2 garlic cloves, finely chopped

4 tablespoons plain/all-purpose flour

2 tablespoons mild curry powder

1 tablespoon garam masala

600 ml/2½ cups chicken stock

¼ dessert apple, peeled, cored and grated

1 tablespoon soy sauce

2 teaspoons Worcestershire sauce

½ teaspoon salt

1 tablespoon runny honey

a pinch of freshly ground black pepper

FOR THE CHICKEN KATSU

4 skinless chicken breasts

50 g/generous ⅓ cup plain/all-purpose flour

1 egg

100 g/2 cups panko breadcrumbs

1 litre/quart vegetable oil

salt and freshly ground black pepper, to season

800 g/6 cups cooked white Japanese rice, to serve

parsley and cherry tomatoes, to garnish (optional)

SERVES 4

For the curry sauce, put the vegetable oil into a large saucepan over a low heat. Add the onion, carrot and garlic and fry gently for about 10 minutes until softened and lightly browned. Add the flour, curry powder and garam masala to the pan and fry for 2 minutes until fragrant. Turn off the heat, then pour in the stock slowly, stirring, to dissolve the curry powder (it may become lumpy if you add the stock too fast). Return to a medium-high heat and bring to the boil. Remove from the heat and blend the curry sauce with a hand blender or in a food processor or blender until smooth. Stir in the grated apple, soy sauce, Worcestershire sauce, salt, honey and black pepper. Place back over a medium heat and simmer for 10 minutes, stirring constantly, until thickened.

Meanwhile, prepare the chicken katsu. Season the chicken breasts with salt and pepper. Prepare a shallow dish each of flour, egg (lightly beaten) and panko breadcrumbs. Coat the chicken breasts first in the flour, then in the beaten egg and finally in the panko breadcrumbs, ensuring the chicken is fully and evenly coated. Refrigerate for 15 minutes to allow the coating to set.

Heat the vegetable oil in a heavy-based saucepan to 170°C (340°F) over a high heat. To check that the oil is ready, drop a few breadcrumbs into the oil. If they float to the surface and sizzle, then it means the oil is ready. Reduce the heat to medium to maintain the temperature. Deep-fry the chicken breasts, two at a time, for about 5 minutes each (depending on the size of your chicken breasts), turning over a few times, until golden brown and crispy and the chicken is cooked through. Remove with a slotted spoon and transfer to a cooling rack. Leave to cool a little, then slice the chicken widthways.

To serve, place the cooked rice onto serving plates and pour over the warm curry sauce. Place the sliced chicken katsu on top of the sauce and garnish each serving with parsley and cherry tomatoes, if liked.

VIETNAMESE CHICKEN CURRY

vegetable oil, for frying

1 red onion, roughly diced

20 g/¾ oz. fresh ginger, peeled and grated

20 g/¾ oz. lemongrass, finely chopped or blended

2 large chicken legs, cut into bite sized pieces, or 6 whole drumsticks, skin on

1 tablespoon curry powder

2 garlic cloves, finely chopped

200 g/7 oz. potatoes, peeled and cubed

90 g/3¼ oz. carrot, cubed

165 ml/⅔ cup coconut milk

300 ml/1¼ cups chicken stock

4 tablespoons fish sauce

1 teaspoon caster/granulated sugar

freshly ground black pepper, to season

90 g/3¼ oz. aubergine/eggplant, cubed (optional)

90 g/3¼ oz. okra, cut into bite-sized pieces (optional)

90 g/3¼ oz. asparagus, cut into bite-sized pieces (optional)

50 g/1¾ oz. mangetouts/snow peas (optional)

15 g/½ oz. Thai basil, to garnish (optional)

15 g/½ oz. spring onion/scallion, thinly sliced on a diagonal, to garnish (optional)

2 bird's eye chillies/chiles, deseeded and sliced, to garnish (optional)

SERVES 2

FRAGRANT VIETNAMESE CURRY IS LIGHT AND MILD, EATEN WITH BAGUETTE TO KICK START THE DAY. IT IS MORE LIKE A STEW WITH CHICKEN, CARROTS, POTATO AND LOTS OF LEMONGRASS AND COCONUT CURRY BROTH TO DIP YOUR BREAD IN. YOU CAN ADD MORE HEAT AND OTHER VEGETABLES TO YOUR LIKING.

Heat the vegetable oil in a medium saucepan and sweat off the red onion, ginger and lemongrass on a medium heat. Once the onion has softened, add the chicken and cook until browned off.

Add the curry powder, stirring well to coat the chicken. Then add the garlic, potatoes, carrot, coconut milk and chicken stock and mix well. Continue to cook with a lid on for about 10 minutes.

Season the curry with the fish sauce, sugar and a pinch of black pepper, then add in the aubergine, okra and any other additional vegetables of your choice. Cook for a further 8–10 minutes.

Garnish with Thai basil, spring onions and a few slices of red bird's eye chilli. Serve with steamed rice or with a fresh baguette and butter.

THAI GREEN CAULI CURRY

2 tablespoons coconut oil

2 tablespoons Green Curry Paste (Page 10)

1 red onion, sliced

4 garlic cloves, minced

200 g/7 oz. tenderstem cauliflower or cauliflower florets

1 red (bell) pepper, deseeded and thinly sliced

2 purple or normal carrots, peeled and sliced on a diagonal

2 baby pak choi/bok choy, halved

100 g/3½ oz. mangetouts/ snow peas

1 tablespoon palm sugar/ jaggery

1 tablespoon liquid aminos (or tamari)

1 x 400-ml/14-oz. can coconut milk

3 makrut lime leaves

freshly squeezed juice of 1 lime

salt and freshly ground black pepper, to season

TO SERVE

a bunch of purple Thai basil

sambal oelek (Asian chilli/chile paste) (optional)

cooked rice

lime wedges

SERVES 4

AROMATIC, CREAMY, FRESH AND ZINGY, JUST LIKE A GOOD THAI CURRY SHOULD BE. THE ADDITION OF LIQUID AMINOS IN PLACE OF THE TRADITIONAL FISH SAUCE ADDS A DEPTH OF FLAVOUR AND EXTRA UMAMI GOODNESS.

In a large frying pan/skillet or wok set over a medium-high heat, heat 1 tablespoon of the coconut oil, being cautious of it spitting. Add the curry paste and fry it, stirring it into the coconut oil, for about 1 minute. Turn the heat down, add the onion and cook until the onion is slightly translucent, about 8 minutes.

Add the garlic, stir together, then add the second tablespoon of coconut oil. Add the cauliflower, red (bell) pepper, carrots, pak choi and mangetouts. Add the palm sugar, liquid aminos (or tamari) and some salt and pepper and stir everything together. Reduce the heat to medium and cook down, stirring, until the carrots are tender-crisp, about 10–15 minutes.

Add the coconut milk and makrut lime leaves, stir, and then let it simmer for about 5 minutes. Squeeze the lime juice over, stir, and then remove from the heat.

Add the purple Thai basil and stir in the sambal oelek, if using. Serve with rice and lime wedges.

CAULIFLOWER KATSU CURRY

5 tablespoons plain/all-purpose flour

1 cauliflower, cut into rounds (steaks)

100 g/2⅓ cups panko breadcrumbs

2 tablespoons vegetable oil, plus extra as needed

1 onion, thinly sliced

2 garlic cloves, finely chopped

5-cm/2-in. piece of fresh ginger, peeled and grated

1 tablespoon curry powder

600 ml/2½ cups vegetable stock

2 tablespoons soy sauce

2 teaspoons runny honey

2 teaspoons rice vinegar

1 teaspoon garam masala

2–3 tablespoons coconut cream

salt and freshly ground black pepper, to season

boiled rice, to serve

micro herbs, to garnish (optional)

FOR THE QUICK PICKLE

1 carrot, peeled and julienned

1–2 mini courgettes/zucchini, thinly sliced on a diagonal

4 radishes, trimmed and sliced

2 tablespoons rice vinegar

1 teaspoon caster/granulated sugar

2 teaspoons sesame seeds

a pinch of salt, to season

SERVES 2

KATSU IS A JAPANESE CURRY AND IS GENERALLY THICKER, MILDER AND SWEETER THAN AN INDIAN CURRY. IT IS TRADITIONALLY SERVED WITH CHICKEN BUT IS ABSOLUTELY DELICIOUS SERVED WITH A BREADED CAULIFLOWER STEAK.

In a large bowl, combine 3 tablespoons of the flour with enough water to make a runny paste, then season and add the cauliflower rounds, tossing until they are all coated. Tip the breadcrumbs onto a plate and dip in each cauliflower round, pressing down to help the crumbs stick all over.

Preheat the oven to 180°C (350°F) Gas 4.

Heat the oil in a frying pan/skillet. Cook the cauliflower in batches for 5 minutes on each side, adding a little more oil between batches if needed. Transfer the slices to a baking sheet as you go. Once all the cauliflower is browned, place the baking sheet in the preheated oven and cook for 10–15 minutes while you make the sauce.

Meanwhile, make the quick pickle. Combine all the ingredients in a bowl with a pinch of salt, and set aside.

Wipe out the frying pan/skillet and heat another drizzle of oil. Add the onion and cook for a few minutes to soften. Stir in the garlic, ginger and curry powder for 1 minute, then add the remaining 2 tablespoons flour. Gently add the stock, little by little, stirring for a smooth sauce. Add the soy sauce, honey, rice vinegar, garam masala and coconut cream, then simmer over a low heat for 10 minutes, adding a splash of water if it gets too thick.

Serve the crispy cauliflower steaks and sauce with boiled rice and the quick pickle on the side. Garnish with micro herbs, if you like.

BEEF STEW WITH STAR ANISE

2 tablespoons vegetable oil

1 teaspoon annatto seeds

1 onion, roughly chopped

450 g/1 lb. braising beef, beef tendons or rib, cubed

2 teaspoons dried chilli flakes/ dried hot pepper flakes

1 teaspoon ground cumin

10 star anise

1 bay leaf

1 teaspoon paprika

½ teaspoon ground cloves

2 garlic cloves, sliced

2.5-cm/1-in. piece of fresh ginger, coarsely chopped

2 lemongrass stalks (outer layer removed), finely chopped

400 ml/1⅔ cups cider (or coconut water, but halve the sugar)

100 ml/⅓ cup chicken or beef stock

2 carrots, roughly sliced

2 potatoes, cubed

2 teaspoons sugar

3 tablespoons fish sauce

1 teaspoon cornflour/cornstarch

130 g/1 cup fresh or frozen peas

freshly ground black pepper, to season

280 g/10 oz. thick rice vermicelli, cooked, or warm baguette and butter (buttered toast also works), to serve

lime wedges

beansprouts, to garnish (optional)

Thai sweet basil, to garnish (optional)

coriander/cilantro, to garnish (optional)

SERVES 4

LEMONGRASS AND STAR ANISE PERFUME THE AIR WHEN THIS IS STEWING ON THE STOVE, MAKING ANY PLACE FEEL LIKE HOME. THE ULTIMATE COMFORT FOOD, BÒ KHO IS SPICY AND FRAGRANT ENOUGH TO AWAKEN THE SENSES AT THE START OF THE DAY. IT IS A THRIFTY DISH DESIGNED TO MAKE USE OF CHEAP CUTS OF BEEF AND WHICHEVER VEGETABLES YOU HAVE THAT NEED TO BE USED UP.

Heat the oil in a large saucepan over a medium heat. Fry the annatto seeds for a couple of minutes until the reddish colour is released. Pour the oil into a bowl and discard the seeds.

In the same pan over a low heat, gently fry the onion until softened. Turn the heat up to high and add the beef. Fry it, turning it often, until browned all over. You may need to do this in batches – if the meat is too cramped, it will stew rather than sear properly.

Add the chilli flakes, cumin, star anise, bay leaf, paprika, cloves, garlic, ginger and lemongrass and pour in the cider, stock and reserved red annatto oil. Stir well. Cover the pan with the lid and cook for about 15 minutes.

Add the carrots and potatoes and season with the sugar and fish sauce. Reduce the heat to low–medium and cook with the lid on for a further 30 minutes.

Put the cornflour and a few drops of water in a small bowl and stir to mix. Add it to the stew, along with the peas, and cook for 5–10 minutes, stirring occasionally, until the sauce has thickened slightly. The beef should be tender, but the cooking time may vary so braise it for longer if it is still tough.

Season with more fish sauce or pepper, to taste, and remove the star anise. Serve with the vermicelli.

To garnish, squeeze lime into the stew. Serve the optional garnishes on the side.

FISH, PUMPKIN & COCONUT CURRY

1 medium pumpkin or squash (about 750 g/2 lbs.), peeled, deseeded and cut into 2.5-cm/1-in. slices

4 tablespoons sunflower/ safflower or groundnut/ peanut oil

5-cm/2-in. piece of fresh ginger, peeled and grated

4 garlic cloves, chopped

a small bunch of coriander/ cilantro, stalks and leaves separated

3–4 red chillies/chiles, deseeded and sliced

1 large onion, halved and sliced

300 g/10 oz. tomatoes, skinned, deseeded and chopped

400 ml/1⅔ cups fish stock

2 green (bell) peppers, deseeded and sliced

1 x 400-ml/14-oz. can coconut milk

2–4 teaspoons tamarind paste

900 g/2 lbs. thick, white fish fillets, cut into chunks

650 g/1½ lbs. uncooked prawns/ shrimp, shelled and deveined

salt and freshly ground black pepper, to season

FOR THE SPICE MIX

4 cloves

1 teaspoon coriander seeds

2 teaspoons cumin seeds

½ teaspoon black peppercorns

1 teaspoon ground turmeric

SERVES 4–6

THE SWEET, RICH FLAVOUR OF ROASTED PUMPKIN WORKS SO WELL WITH THE SPICES IN THIS LIGHT, FRAGRANT CURRY. THE FISH YOU USE NEEDS TO BE ONE THAT WILL CUT INTO CHUNKS AND NOT BREAK UP ON COOKING – MONKFISH IS GOOD. SERVE WITH A GREEN VEGETABLE, STIR-FRIED WITH ONION, GINGER AND KALONJI (NIGELLA) SEEDS AND SOME SAFFRON RICE.

Preheat the oven to 200°C (400°F) Gas 6. Toss the pumpkin with 2 tablespoons of the oil and some salt and pepper. Transfer to a baking tray and roast in the preheated oven, stirring once or twice, until browned and tender, about 35–40 minutes.

Meanwhile, for the spice mix, in a small dry, frying pan/skillet over medium heat, toast the cloves, coriander seeds and half the cumin seeds for 2–3 minutes until fragrant. Let cool, then grind in a mill or mortar and pestle with the black peppercorns to make a powder. Stir in the ground turmeric.

Blend together the ginger, garlic, coriander stalks and 2–3 chillies with 3 tablespoons water to form a paste, then blend in 2 teaspoons of the dry spice mixture.

In a saucepan, very gently fry the onion in the remaining oil with a pinch of salt for 10 minutes until softened but not browned. Add the remaining cumin seeds and fry for another 3–4 minutes, then add the ginger paste, turn up the heat and stir-fry for 4–5 minutes until the liquid evaporates. Add the tomatoes and cook again for 3–4 minutes until the mixture looks dry. Stir in the stock and peppers and cook for 10 minutes. Add the coconut milk and 2 teaspoons tamarind. Let it bubble gently for a few minutes, then stir in seasoning and more tamarind to taste. Stir in the pumpkin and fish and let it gently cook for 5 minutes then add the prawns and cook until they turn pink.

Add more of the spice mixture to taste, stir in most of the chopped coriander leaves and transfer to a serving dish. Sprinkle with the remaining coriander and red chilli, thinly sliced. Serve immediately.

GREEN COCONUT & PRAWN/ SHRIMP CURRY

DELICATELY PERFUMED WITH MAKRUT LIME LEAVES AND LEMONGRASS, THIS CURRY IS GIVEN A LITTLE KICK WITH THE ADDITION OF GREEN PEPPERCORNS AND FRESH CHILLIES/CHILES.

2 tablespoons coconut oil

2 tablespoons Green Curry Paste (page 10)

820 ml/3½ cups coconut milk

45 g/1 cup dried unsweetened coconut flakes

450 g/1 lb. uncooked prawns/ shrimp, shelled and deveined, tails on

freshly chopped coriander/ cilantro, to serve

makrut or regular limes, to serve

SERVES 4

Set a deep frying pan/skillet over a medium-high heat and add the coconut oil. Add the curry paste and cook for 3–4 minutes, stirring continuously. Add the coconut milk and flakes to the pan and stir to combine. Bring to the boil, then reduce the heat and simmer for 20 minutes.

Increase the heat and bring the mixture back to the boil. Add the prawns, cover and cook for 5–6 minutes until they are pink and cooked through. Remove from the heat and rest for 5 minutes.

Spoon into bowls and sprinkle with coriander leaves. Serve with limes to squeeze.

ASIAN BEEF BRAISE WITH PAK CHOI/ BOK CHOY

A DIFFERENT KIND OF BEEF STEW, THIS RECIPE HAS FLAVOURS OF THE ORIENT BUT IS EASY TO MAKE AT HOME WITH ORDINARY WESTERN UTENSILS. IF YOU CAN FIND CUBES OF FROZEN CHOPPED GINGER AT YOUR SUPERMARKET, THEY WILL COME IN HANDY HERE. SERVE THIS WITH ANY KIND OF ORIENTAL NOODLE – EGG NOODLES WILL DO THE TRICK, OR TRY SOMETHING UNUSUAL LIKE JAPANESE SOBA NOODLES OR THICK HO FUN NOODLES.

2 tablespoons vegetable oil

1 kg/1¼ lbs. braising steak, cut into bite-sized pieces

1 garlic clove, minced

1 large shallot, sliced

2.5-cm/1-in. piece of fresh ginger, peeled and grated

750 ml/3 cups beef stock

125 ml/½ cup Chinese rice wine

125 ml/½ cup hoisin sauce

¼ teaspoon ground cumin

1 star anise

1 fresh red chilli/chile, deseeded and sliced

freshly squeezed juice of 1 tangerine (or ½ an orange)

1 teaspoon runny honey

4–6 pak-choi/bok choy

noodles of choice, to serve

SERVES 4

Heat the oil in a large saucepan. Add the steak and cook until browned. Transfer to a plate, season with salt and set aside.

Add the garlic, shallot and ginger to the saucepan and cook, stirring constantly for 1 minute. Add the stock, rice wine, hoisin sauce, cumin, star anise, chilli, tangerine juice and honey. Stir to blend and bring to the boil. Return the steak to the saucepan, reduce the heat and simmer very gently, uncovered, for 1–1½ hours, until the meat is tender. Taste and adjust the seasoning.

Core the pak-choi/bok choy. Cut the white part into 1.5-cm/½-in. slices; leave the greens large or cut in half. Add the white part to the saucepan, increase the heat and cook until just tender, 3–4 minutes. Add the greens and cook until just wilted, about 2–3 minutes more. Serve immediately with cooked noodles of choice.

WHITE FISH, SOYA BEAN/ SOYBEAN & BABY CARROT HOTPOT

IF YOU HAPPEN TO LIVE IN A CITY WHICH HAS A CHINATOWN OR EVEN AN ASIAN SPECIALITY FOOD SHOP, DO LOOK OUT FOR CHINESE EARTHENWARE POTS (SAND POTS). MADE FROM CLAY AND GLAZED INSIDE, THEY CAN BE USED ON BOTH HOB AND IN THE OVEN, JUST LIKE A CONVENTIONAL CASSEROLE, AND ARE PERFECT FOR RECIPES SUCH AS THIS ONE.

800 g/1¾ lb. skinless white fish fillet, cut into bite-sized pieces

60 g/½ cup plain/all-purpose flour

2 tablespoons vegetable oil

2 teaspoons sesame oil

4 garlic cloves, roughly chopped

2 spring onions/scallions, thinly sliced on a diagonal, whites and green parts seperated

1 tablespoon fresh ginger, peeled and grated

8 baby carrots or 1 large carrot, cut into bite-sized pieces

500 ml/2 cups fish or vegetable stock

1 tablespoon Thai fish sauce

1 x 400-g/14-oz. can soya beans/soybeans, rinsed and drained

freshly chopped leaves from a small bunch of coriander/ cilantro

a large flameproof casserole or sand pot

SERVES 4

Put the fish pieces in a sieve/strainer with the flour. Toss to coat the fish in the flour and set aside.

Heat both the oils in a large, flameproof casserole or sand pot set over a high heat. Add the fish pieces in batches, cooking for just 1 minute on each side, until golden. Transfer the fish to a plate as you go.

Add the garlic, spring onion whites and ginger to the casserole and stir-fry for 2 minutes, scraping the base to remove any stuck-on bits. Add the carrots, stock, fish sauce and soya beans. Increase the heat and bring to the boil. Cook for 10 minutes, until the liquid has slightly reduced.

Add the fish pieces and gently stir. Reduce the heat to a low simmer and cook for 5 minutes, until the fish is opaque and cooked through.

Stir in half of the coriander and scatter the remaining coriander and spring onion greens over the top. Serve immediately.

Vegetarian option: Replace the fish with about 200 g/7 oz. peeled, deseeded and chopped butternut squash and 200 g/ 1 cup sliced fresh mushrooms, shiitake if available. Increase the cooking time by 5–10 minutes and cook until the squash is just tender. Use vegetable stock and omit the fish sauce.

CHAPTER ☀ 6

MAIN PLATES

SWEET & SOUR PORK
WITH PINEAPPLE & CUCUMBER

A WORLD AWAY FROM THE LOCAL TAKEAWAY'S GREASY BATTERED NUGGETS DROWNED IN A FLUORESCENT GLOOP, THIS SCRUMPTIOUS RECIPE USES LEAN PORK FILLET, WOK-FRIED WITH CUCUMBER WEDGES AND JUICY PINEAPPLE CHUNKS AND LIGHTLY COATED IN A SWEET AND TANGY SAUCE.

600 g/1 lb. 4 oz. pork fillet, cut into 2.5-cm/1-in. chunks

1 tablespoon light soy sauce

2 teaspoons fresh ginger, peeled and grated

2 tablespoons vegetable oil

1 large red (bell) pepper, deseeded and cut into 2.5-cm/1-in. chunks

1 large onion, cut into 8 wedges

½ large cucumber, roughly peeled, halved, deseeded and thickly sliced

300 g/10 oz. fresh or tinned pineapple, cut into 2-cm/1-in. chunks

cooked rice or noodles, to serve

FOR THE SAUCE

100 ml/⅓ cup pure pineapple juice

4 tablespoons tomato ketchup

2 tablespoons rice vinegar

1 tablespoon light soy sauce

1 tablespoon caster/granulated sugar

1 tablespoon cornflour/cornstarch

SERVES 4

Combine all the sauce ingredients in a bowl and set aside.

Put the pork, soy sauce and ginger in a bowl and mix well. Cover and marinate in the fridge for 20 minutes, if possible.

Heat the oil in a wok or large frying pan/skillet until hot, then add the pork in batches (don't overcrowd the wok, otherwise the pork will stew rather than fry). Stir-fry over a high heat for 4–5 minutes until nearly cooked through and well-sealed all over. Remove the pork from the wok and set aside.

Throw the red (bell) pepper and onion into the wok and stir-fry for 2–3 minutes. Return the pork to the wok with any juices. Pour in the sauce and toss everything together. Bring to the boil, then reduce the heat.

Add the cucumber and pineapple and simmer gently for 3–4 minutes, or until the sauce has thickened and the pork is cooked through. Divide between four bowls and serve immediately with rice or noodles.

SZECHUAN ROASTED PORK BELLY WITH PLUMS

PORK BELLY IS A DELICIOUS TREAT. SLOWLY ROAST IT TO A DARK, CRISPY CRUST AND THEN TOP WITH SWEET, JUICY PLUMS. IN WINTER SERVE IT WITH NOODLES OR RICE, AND IN SUMMER KEEP IT SIMPLE WITH A LARGE, CRISP GREEN SALAD. ALLOW PLENTY OF MARINATING TIME FOR THE BEST FLAVOUR.

a 1.5-kg/3½-lb. piece of pork belly

2 teaspoons salt

70 g/¼ cup orange-blossom honey

60 ml/¼ cup soy sauce

60 ml/¼ cup rice wine vinegar

1 tablespoon toasted sesame oil

1 tablespoon sambal oelek (Asian chilli/chile paste)

1 tablespoon crushed Szechuan peppercorns

4 garlic cloves

5-cm/2-in. piece of fresh ginger, peeled

½ teaspoon ground cinnamon

6 medium plums, halved and pitted

SERVES 6

Put the pork belly on a work surface. Score the skin and rub all over with the salt.

Put the honey, soy sauce, vinegar, sesame oil, sambal oelek, peppercorns, garlic, ginger and cinnamon in a blender and process until smooth. Pour the mixture into a baking dish and lay the pork on top, skin-side down. Spoon the mixture over the pork to coat evenly. Cover and refrigerate for 6–24 hours.

Remove the pork from the fridge, uncover and bring to room temperature.

Preheat the oven to 175°C (350°F) Gas 4.

Place the pork in the oven and roast for 2 hours, basting every 30 minutes.

Remove the pork from the oven and drain off the excess fat. Turn the pork skin-side up in the pan so that it crisps. Arrange the plums around the pork and return to the oven for 30–40 minutes.

Remove from the oven and tent with foil. Rest for 15 minutes. To serve, cut into thick slices and top with the roasted plums.

CHAR-GRILLED TAMARIND PRAWNS/SHRIMP

THIS IS POPULAR STREET FOOD IN MALAYSIA AND INDONESIA. THE AROMA
EMANATING FROM THE STALLS AS THE MARINATED PRAWNS/SHRIMP
ARE GRILLED OVER CHARCOAL MAKES YOU FEEL VERY HUNGRY.

500 g/1 lb. 2 oz. uncooked large/
jumbo prawns/shrimp,
shelled, deveined and
trimmed of heads, feelers
and legs

FOR THE MARINADE

3 tablespoons tamarind pulp*

250 ml/1 cup warm water

2 tablespoons sweet soy sauce

1 tablespoon caster/granulated
sugar

freshly ground black pepper

TO SERVE

leaves from a small bunch of
fresh coriander/cilantro

2–4 fresh green chillies/chiles,
deseeded and sliced

a packet of wooden or bamboo
skewers, soaked in water
before use

SERVES 2–4

Rinse the prepared prawns well, pat dry and using a very sharp
knife, make an incision along the curve of the tail. Set aside.

Put the tamarind pulp in a bowl and add the warm water.
Soak the pulp, until soft, squeezing it with your fingers to help
dissolve it. Strain the liquid and discard any fibre or seeds.
In a bowl, mix together the tamarind juice, soy sauce, sugar
and black pepper. Pour it over the prawns, rubbing it over the
shells and into the incision in the tails. Cover, refrigerate and
leave to marinate for about 1 hour.

Insert a skewer into each marinated prawn. Prepare a charcoal
or conventional grill. Cook the prawns for about 3 minutes on
each side, until the prawn shells have turned orange, brushing
them with the marinade as they cook. Serve immediately,
garnished with the coriander leaves and chillies.

Note: Tamarind lends a rich, sweet-sour flavour to dishes.
The tropical trees produce fresh pods that are either sold fresh
or processed into pulp or paste for convenience and long
shelf life. You may think you've never tried tamarind;
however, it is an essential ingredient in several traditional
British condiments, most notably brown sauce. Look out for
it in Caribbean markets – semi-dried tamarind pulp comes
in soft rectangular blocks wrapped in plastic. The darker
concentrated paste is sold in tubs and is a more
processed product.

MISO & NUT-CRUSTED SALMON

MISO IS A TRADITIONAL STAPLE OF JAPANESE COOKING. IT IS MADE BY
FERMENTING SOYA BEANS IN SEA SALT, WHICH RESULTS IN A THICK PASTE.
MOST COMMON ARE WHITE, YELLOW AND RED MISO. THE DELICATE, SLIGHTLY
SALTY AND FRUITY FLAVOUR OF YELLOW MISO REALLY ENHANCES THE FLAVOUR
OF WILD SALMON. THIS IS A FANTASTIC EASY SUPPER DISH AND HEALTHY, TOO.

2 x 225 g/8 oz. wild salmon
fillets, centre cut

1 tablespoon olive oil

chopped chives, to garnish

FOR THE MISO & NUT TOPPING

1 tablespoon yellow miso paste

60 g/½ cup cashews, roughly
chopped

½ red Serrano chilli/chile,
deseeded and finely chopped

finely grated zest and freshly
squeezed juice of 1 lime

1 tablespoon toasted sesame oil

SERVES 2

Preheat the oven to 200°C (400°F) Gas 6.

Rinse and dry the salmon. Drizzle the olive oil into a small
baking dish and place the salmon fillets in it.

To make the topping, mix together the miso, cashews, chilli,
lime zest and juice and sesame oil. Divide the mixture and
spread on top of the salmon fillets.

Cook in the preheated oven for 12–15 minutes until the fish
is cooked and the topping is golden brown.

Garnish with chopped chives and serve.

TUNA CARPACCIO & COURGETTE/ ZUCCHINI RIBBONS
WITH SOY & SESAME DRESSING

a 400-g/14-oz. piece of tuna
in a neat 'log', trimmed
of all skin

2 tablespoons freshly chopped
coriander/cilantro

salt and freshly ground black
pepper, to season

vegetable oil, for frying

FOR THE DRESSING AND SALAD

4 tablespoons olive oil or
groundnut/peanut oil

1 garlic clove, minced

grated zest and freshly squeezed
juice of 1 lime

½–1 teaspoon red chilli/chile,
deseeded and sliced (optional)

a 3–4-cm/1½-in. piece of fresh
ginger, peeled and grated

½ teaspoon runny honey

soy sauce and toasted sesame
oil, to taste

4 small courgettes/zucchini,
topped and tailed

a small handful of sprouted
seeds or shoots, such as cress,
coriander/cilantro, alfalfa or
pea shoots

a handful of peppery salad
leaves, such as rocket/
arugula, baby mustard and
mizuna

toasted sesame seeds, to serve

SERVES 4

THE SWEET, NUTTY CRUNCH OF RAW COURGETTES/ZUCCHINI
WORKS WELL WITH THE SMOOTH TEXTURE OF WAFER-THIN
SLICES OF TUNA, MAKING THIS A GREAT SUMMER DISH,
AS YOUNG COURGETTES/ZUCCHINI ARE AT THEIR SWEETEST
THEN. IT GOES WITHOUT SAYING THAT YOU SHOULD SEEK
OUT THE BEST, FRESHEST TUNA YOU CAN FIND.

Rub the tuna with a few drops of oil and season well. Heat
a ridged griddle pan or non-stick frying pan/skillet over a high
heat until very hot, then sear the tuna quickly on all sides.
It should brown on the outside, but appear cooked for only
5 mm/⅛ in. around the edge. Remove from the heat, let cool
a little, then roll the tuna in the chopped coriander to cover. Let
cool completely, wrap in clingfilm/plastic wrap and chill well
in the fridge.

Meanwhile, put the oil for the dressing in a bowl and add the
garlic, a pinch or two of grated lime zest and the chilli (if using).
Leave on one side while the tuna chills. Heat about 5 mm/¼ in.
of oil in a small frying pan/skillet over a medium heat. When hot,
add the ginger and cook briefly (30–60 seconds) until golden and
crisp. Drain on paper towels.

When ready to serve, remove and discard the garlic from the
dressing, then whisk in the honey and 2 teaspoons lime juice.
Add a few drops of soy and sesame oil to taste and season with
salt, pepper and more lime juice.

Unwrap the tuna, cut wafer-thin slices across the grain and lay
these, overlapping, on four plates. Using a vegetable peeler,
cut long, thin ribbons of courgette, directly into a salad bowl.
Add the sprouts and the salad leaves and toss with most of the
dressing. Add a pile of salad to each plate, sprinkle over the fried
ginger and sesame seeds, drizzle with the remaining dressing and
serve immediately.

CITRUS AHI TUNA
WITH YUZU DIPPING SAUCE

BUY SUSHI-GRADE AHI (OR YELLOWFIN) TUNA TO MAKE THIS DISH AND WRAP
IT UP IN A CITRUSY PEPPER CRUST. THE LEMONY YUZU JUICE IS A MUST, BUT
IF YOU CAN'T FIND IT YOU CAN USE LEMON JUICE. SHISO IS A WONDERFUL
CITRUS FLAVOURED HERB, BUT YOU COULD USE OTHER LEAVES, SUCH AS BASIL.

450 g/1 lb. sushi-grade ahi
(or yellowfin) tuna

2 teaspoons finely chopped
dried orange peel

4 teaspoons ground green
peppercorns

1 teaspoon salt

2 tablespoons sunflower/
safflower oil

shiso leaves, to serve (optional)

DIPPING SAUCE

1 tablespoon yuzu juice

2 teaspoons sesame oil

1 tablespoon soy sauce

1 teaspoon fresh ginger, peeled
and grated

1 teaspoon green chilli/chile,
deseeded and sliced

a pinch of brown sugar

SERVES 2

To make the dipping sauce, whisk all the ingredients together.
Pour into a bowl and set aside.

Rinse the tuna under cold running water and pat dry. Cut it into
two rectangles and set aside.

Mix the orange peel, peppercorns and salt together on a large
plate, then roll the tuna in the mix to completely cover.

Set a large frying pan/skillet over a medium–high heat and pour
in the oil. When the pan is smoking, add the tuna and sear
on all sides for about 3 minutes in total. You want the middle
of the tuna to remain raw.

Transfer the tuna from the pan to a cutting board and rest
for a few minutes. Place a few shiso leaves on two plates. Cut
the tuna into slices 2.5 cm/1 in. thick and arrange on the leaves.
Serve with the dipping sauce.

TOFU & TOMATOES IN FISH SAUCE

THIS VERY PLAIN AND UNCOMPLEX RECIPE IS DECEPTIVE IN ITS MODESTY BECAUSE IT IS REALLY TASTY! HERBS, FRUITS AND VEGETABLES GROW IN ABUNDANCE IN VIETNAM, SO SIDE DISHES SUCH AS THIS CAN ACCOMPANY FISH AND MEAT DISHES.

250 g/9 oz. fresh tofu, cut into 9 cubes

2½ tablespoons vegetable oil

1 garlic clove, minced

1 Asian shallot, finely chopped

3 tomatoes, quartered

2 spring onions/scallions, thinly sliced on a diagonal

2 tablespoons mirin

1 tablespoon fish sauce

cooked rice or rice vermicelli, to serve (optional)

mint or hot mint, Thai sweet basil or coriander/cilantro, to garnish (optional)

SERVES 2–3

Pat the tofu dry. Heat 2 tablespoons of the oil in a frying pan/skillet over a medium heat and fry the tofu until golden all over – about 7 minutes. Remove from the heat and place on paper towels to soak up the excess oil.

Heat the remaining oil in the frying pan and fry the garlic and shallots until softened, then add the tomatoes and spring onions. Don't stir the tomatoes for a couple of minutes to encourage them to brown on one side, then gently turn them over. Fry for about 4 minutes.

Add the tofu, the mirin and fish sauce and fry for 2–3 minutes, stirring gently.

Serve with cooked rice or rice vermicelli. Garnish with garden or hot mint, Thai sweet basil or coriander, if you like.

STICKY SESAME AUBERGINE
WITH GOCHUJANG KETCHUP

SPOON INTO WARM PITTA BREAD, WITH CRISP SHREDDED LETTUCE AND
GOCHUJANG KETCHUP.

2 medium aubergines/eggplants

2 tablespoons sesame oil

2 tablespoons olive oil

4-cm/1½-in. piece of fresh ginger, peeled and grated

4 tablespoons *ketjap manis* (thick, sweet Indonesian soy sauce)

120 ml/½ cup dark soy sauce

4 teaspoons gochujang paste

2 teaspoons caster/granulated sugar

3 garlic cloves, minced

2–3 tablespoons sesame seeds

a bunch of spring onions/ scallions, thinly sliced on a diagonal

FOR THE GOCHUJANG KETCHUP

4 tablespoons gochujang paste

4 tablespoons good-quality tomato ketchup

TO SERVE

4 pitta breads, warmed

shredded lettuce

SERVES 4

Preheat the oven to 190°C (375°F) Gas 5.

Cut the aubergines into bite-sized cubes and transfer them to a large bowl.

In a separate bowl, mix the sesame oil, olive oil, grated ginger, *ketjap manis*, soy sauce, 4 teaspoons gochujang paste, sugar and garlic. Stir everything together and pour the mixture over the aubergine cubes. Toss to coat everything well.

Spoon the aubergine evenly over a large, flat sheet pan and roast for about 25–30 minutes, until the aubergine is cooked. Scatter over the sesame seeds and chopped spring onions.

To make the gochujang ketchup, simply mix the gochujang paste with the tomato ketchup in a small bowl.

Scoop the aubergine mixture into warmed pitta breads, and add shredded lettuce and gochujang ketchup, as desired.

SPICY MAPLE BAKED TOFU
WITH BUCKWHEAT NOODLES

I LOVE THE SLIGHT SWEETNESS OF THE MAPLE SYRUP COMBINED WITH THE
EARTHINESS OF THE SPICE, THEN TOPPED WITH A BREATH OF THE OCEAN
WITH NORI SEAWEED. SERVE THE TOFU WARM OR CHILLED – EITHER WAY
IT'S HEAVEN IN A BOWL.

450 g/1 lb. firm organic tofu

70 ml/⅓ cup good-quality
maple syrup

1 tablespoon olive oil

2 teaspoons smoked pimentón

1 teaspoon freshly cracked
Tellicherry pepper

a pinch of salt

270 g/9½ oz. buckwheat soba
noodles

tamari or soy sauce, to drizzle

1 sheet of nori seaweed,
crumbled or finely sliced

SERVES 4

Preheat the oven to 200°C (400°F) Gas 6.

Slice the tofu into pieces 1 cm/½ in. thick and arrange
in a single layer in a ceramic baking dish.

In a medium bowl whisk together the maple syrup, olive oil,
smoked pimentón, pepper and salt. Pour over the tofu to coat,
then bake in the preheated oven for 30 minutes.

Bring a large pan of water to boil over a high heat and add the
noodles. Cook for 4 minutes, then drain, rinse under cold water
and set aside.

To serve, divide the noodles between four bowls and drizzle
with a touch of tamari or soy sauce. Top with a couple
of pieces of tofu and sprinkle with a little of the seaweed.

DUCK SATAY WITH GRILLED PINEAPPLE & PLUM SAUCE

CHICKEN SATAYS ARE POPULAR THROUGHOUT SOUTHEAST ASIA BUT
IN VIETNAM, CAMBODIA AND CHINA, DUCK SATAYS ARE COMMON TOO.
DUCK IS OFTEN SERVED IN THE CHINESE TRADITION OF SWEET AND SOUR
WITH A FRUITY SAUCE. YOU CAN BUY READY-MADE BOTTLED PLUM SAUCE
IN CHINESE MARKETS AND MOST STORES.

700 g/1 lb. 9 oz. duck breasts
or boned thighs, sliced into
thin, bite-sized strips

1–2 tablespoons groundnut/
peanut or coconut oil, for
brushing

1 small pineapple, peeled,
cored and sliced

Chinese plum sauce, to serve

FOR THE MARINADE

2–3 tablespoons light soy sauce

freshly squeezed juice of 1 lime

1–2 teaspoons caster/
granulated sugar

1–2 garlic cloves, minced

25 g/1 oz. fresh ginger, peeled
and grated

1 small onion, grated

1–2 teaspoons ground
coriander/cilantro

1 teaspoon salt

a packet of wooden or bamboo
skewers, soaked in water
before use

SERVES 4

To make the marinade, put the soy sauce and lime juice
in a bowl with the sugar and mix until it dissolves. Add the
garlic, ginger and grated onion and stir in the coriander
and salt.

Place the strips of duck in a bowl and pour over the marinade.
Toss well, cover and chill in the refrigerator for at least 4 hours.

Thread the duck strips onto the skewers and brush them
with oil.

Prepare a charcoal or conventional grill/broiler.

Cook the satays for 3–4 minutes on each side, until the duck
is nicely browned. Grill the slices of pineapple at the same time.
When browned, cut them into bite-sized pieces and serve with
the duck. Drizzle with the plum sauce to serve.

SWEET & SOUR ORANGE CHICKEN WITH PINEAPPLE FRIED RICE

THIS DISH COMBINES TWO DELICIOUS DISHES THAT ARE JUST TOO HARD TO CHOOSE BETWEEN IN A CHINESE RESTAURANT!

675 g/1½ lbs. boneless skinless chicken, chopped into bite-sized pieces

2 eggs

1 teaspoon salt

ground white pepper, to taste

1 litre/quart groundnut/peanut oil, for frying

40 g/⅓ cup cornflour/cornstarch, plus 1 tablespoon for thickening

35 g/¼ cup plain/all-purpose flour

4 rings fresh (or canned) pineapple, drained (juice reserved)

1 tablespoon fresh ginger, peeled and grated

1 teaspoon garlic, minced

2 green (bell) peppers, in small pieces

½ tablespoon chilli flakes/hot red pepper flakes

2 spring onions/scallions, thinly sliced on a diagonal

1 tablespoon rice wine

store-bought sweet & sour sauce, to serve

FOR THE PINEAPPLE FRIED RICE

8 rings fresh (or canned) pineapple, drained

2 tablespoons canola oil

1 teaspoon garlic, minced

1 teaspoon fresh ginger, peeled and grated

½ onion, chopped

1 red (bell) pepper, chopped

½ carrot, grated

240 g/2 cups cooked rice

1–2 tablespoons light soy sauce

1 teaspoon Madras curry powder

caster/granulated sugar, to taste

1 spring onion/scallion, thinly sliced on a diagonal

SERVES 4

Place the chicken pieces in a large bowl. Be sure to handle raw chicken with care. In another large bowl, stir together the eggs, salt, pepper and 1 tablespoon of the oil. Mix well. In a small bowl, whisk the 40 g/⅓ cup cornflour/cornstarch and flour together. Mix the flour mixture into egg mixture. Add the chicken pieces, tossing to coat.

Heat the rest of the oil in a large frying pan/skillet, wok or deep-fryer to 190°C (375°F) or until the oil is bubbling steadily. Add the chicken pieces, a few at a time. Fry for 3–4 minutes or until golden crisp.

Remove the chicken from the oil with a slotted spoon; drain on paper towels then set aside. Clean the wok or frying pan/skillet and heat for 15 seconds over a high heat. Add a little oil and then add the ginger and garlic. Stir-fry for 10 seconds or until fragrant. Add the peppers, chilli flakes, spring onions, and rice wine. Stir for a few seconds. Add the sweet and sour sauce and bring to the boil. Add the cooked chicken, stirring until well mixed.

Stir 60 ml/1 cup water into the extra 1 tablespoon cornflour until smooth and add to the chicken. Heat until the sauce has thickened and then turn off the gas.

To make the pineapple fried rice, cut the pineapple rings into small wedges. Heat a wok or frying pan/skillet over a medium heat. Add the oil. When the oil is hot, add the garlic and ginger. Stir-fry for 30 seconds. Add the onion. Stir-fry for 1 minute, then add the red (bell) pepper, grated carrot and pineapple. Mix everything together and then add the cooked rice and fry for 2 minutes. Stir the mixture and toss in the pan until it looks shiny. Add the soy sauce and stir in. Stir in the curry powder and sugar. Stir in the spring onion or use as a garnish.

CRISPY ROAST DUCK & ASIAN GREENS

1 fresh duck, 1.4 kg/3 lbs.

3 tablespoons kosher salt

FOR THE HONEY GLAZE

4 star anise, crushed

100 ml/⅓ cup plus 1 tablespoon runny honey

1 teaspoon ground cinnamon

finely grated zest of 1 orange and freshly squeezed juice of ½ orange (reserve both orange halves for stuffing the duck)

1 teaspoon Sichuan crushed peppercorns

2 tablespoons soy sauce

2.5-cm/1-in. piece fresh of ginger, peeled and grated

2 red Thai chillies/chiles, deseeded and sliced

2 tablespoons dark brown sugar

FOR THE ASIAN GREENS

3 tablespoons groundnut/ peanut oil

2 tablespoons toasted sesame oil

2 tablespoons red wine vinegar

1 teaspoon soy sauce

1 teaspoon runny honey

350 g/3 cups mixed salad greens

freshly ground black pepper and green tea salt, to season

a roasting pan lined with foil

a roasting rack

SERVES 4

RUBBING KOSHER SALT OVER THE DUCK DRAWS EXCESS MOISTURE OUT OF THE SKIN, WHILE SCALDING MAKES FOR A CRISPY SKIN WHEN ROASTED. A WONDERFUL HONEY-SPICED GLAZE ADDS A VIBRANT COLOUR AND FLAVOUR TO THE MEAT.

Wash and dry the duck. Rub the kosher salt all over the duck skin, cover, and leave in the refrigerator overnight.

Put the roasting rack on the lined roasting pan. Bring a kettle of water to the boil. Put the duck in a large bowl and pour boiling water over it. Immediately remove the duck from the bowl and place on the roasting rack in the roasting pan. Set aside.

Preheat the oven to 200°C (400°F) Gas 6.

Stuff the duck with the orange halves. Mix all the glaze ingredients together in a bowl and brush over the duck. Roast in the preheated oven for 30 minutes.

Remove from the oven, and drain off the fat that has accumulated in the bottom of the pan. You may need to cover the tips of the wings with foil, as they will be very crispy. Turn the oven down to 190°C (375°F) Gas 5 and put the duck back in the oven for another 30 minutes.

Remove the duck from the oven and leave it to rest for 15 minutes in a warm place.

To prepare the Asian greens, whisk the groundnut/peanut oil, sesame oil, red wine vinegar, soy sauce and honey together. Season with the cracked black pepper and green tea salt. Put the salad greens in a bowl and toss with the dressing.

Carve the duck and serve with the salad.

THAI-SPICED RARE BEEF & WARM RICE NOODLE SALAD

400 g/14 oz. fillet steak/beef tenderloin

1 tablespoon sunflower/safflower oil

100 g/3½ oz. bamboo shoots, finely shredded

100 g/⅔ cup roasted salted peanuts, coarsely ground

200 g/7 oz. baby spinach leaves

500 g/1 lb. thin rice noodles

1 teaspoon toasted sesame oil

8 spring onions/scallions, thinly sliced on a diagonal

3 tablespoons nuoc cham

2 handfuls of freshly chopped coriander/cilantro

2–3 baby courgettes/zucchini (about 200 g/7 oz.), sliced into ribbons with a mandolin

freshly squeezed juice of ½ lime

a pinch of salt

2 thin red chillies/chiles, deseeded and sliced

FOR THE MARINADE

1 lemongrass stalk, very finely chopped

2 teaspoons Red Curry Paste (page 11)

2 teaspoons nam pla fish sauce

freshly squeezed juice of ½ lime

SERVES 4

THIS RECIPE MAKES A DELICIOUSLY DIFFERENT AND TASTY ORIENTAL VARIATION ON A SIMPLE SALAD.

To make the marinade, mix the lemongrass, curry paste, fish sauce and lime juice, then place the beef in a shallow dish and cover with the marinade. Cover and refrigerate for as long as possible (30 minutes is OK; overnight would be superb).

Heat the oil in a frying pan/skillet over a medium heat and fry the marinated beef (reserving any remaining marinade) for 2 minutes each side. Remove from the pan, cover and set aside. In the same pan, quickly fry the bamboo shoots and peanuts with any remaining marinade. Add the spinach to the pan, immediately remove from the heat and cover with a lid to allow the spinach to wilt in the residual heat.

Blanch the noodles in a pan of boiling water for 5 minutes or until cooked. Drain and toss in the sesame oil, spring onions, nuoc cham and half the coriander. Meanwhile, thinly slice the beef and keep warm.

Dress the courgettes with the lime juice, the remaining coriander and the salt.

To assemble, divide the noodles between four warm plates, then pile the remaining ingredients on top. Garnish with the sliced chillies.

KOREAN STICKY RIBS

GOCHUJANG IS A RED PEPPER PASTE USED IN KOREAN COOKING. IT COMES IN
VARYING DEGREES OF HEAT, SO MAKE SURE TO CHECK THE LABEL AND CHOOSE
SOMETHING TO SUIT YOUR TASTEBUDS. THESE RIBS ARE GREAT FOR THE
BARBECUE/OUTDOOR GRILL; SERVE THEM WITH AN ASIAN COLESLAW OR KIMCHI.

8 Korean-style beef ribs, 1 cm/
  ½ in. thick

3 spring onions/scallions, thinly
  sliced on a diagonal

2 tablespoons black sesame
  seeds

FOR THE MARINADE

60 ml/¼ cup soy sauce

60 ml/¼ cup toasted sesame oil

140 g/½ cup orange-blossom
  honey

2 heaped tablespoons
  gochujang or sambal oelek
  (Asian chilli/chile paste)

1 tablespoon fish sauce

4 garlic cloves, minced

2 Serrano chillies/chiles,
  deseeded and sliced

2 teaspoons cracked rainbow
  peppercorns

½ teaspoon salt

SERVES 4

Lay the ribs in a single layer in a ceramic baking dish.

Put all the marinade ingredients in a blender and process until
smooth. Pour over the ribs and sprinkle with the spring onions
and sesame seeds. Cover and refrigerate for 6–24 hours.

Remove the ribs from the fridge and bring to room temperature.

Heat a grill/broiler or barbecue/outdoor grill to a medium–high
heat. Place the ribs on the rack (reserving the marinade) and
cook for 5 minutes, then turn over and cook for another
5 minutes. Transfer to a warm plate and tent with foil.
Rest for 10 minutes.

Put the remaining marinade in a small saucepan and bring
to the boil, then reduce the heat and simmer for 5 minutes.
To serve, pour the marinade into a bowl and serve alongside
the ribs.

CHAPTER ✲ 7

SWEET THINGS

TOFU NO YAKI CHEESECAKE

ADDING TOFU TO THIS BAKED CHEESECAKE RECIPE KEEPS IT LIGHT AND MOIST – EACH MOUTHFUL ALMOST MELTS IN THE MOUTH. THE TOUCH OF CINNAMON AND ADDITION OF LEMON ZEST MAKES IT THE PERFECT DESSERT TO COMFORT YOU WHEN THE COLDER DAYS ARRIVE. PERFECT FOR EATING WHILE CURLED UP IN A COSY ARMCHAIR WITH A HOT CUP OF TEA!

BASE

160 g/5¾ oz. digestive biscuits/
  graham crackers
60 g/½ stick butter, melted
1 teaspoon ground cinnamon

CHEESECAKE

350 g/12 oz. firm tofu
500 g/2¼ cups soft cheese
175 g/¾ cup plus 2 tablespoons
  caster/granulated sugar
2 large eggs
finely grated zest of 1 lemon
seeds scraped from 1 vanilla
  pod/bean
200 g/7 oz. mixed fresh berries,
  to decorate

20-cm/8-inch round loose-based
cake pan

SERVES 6–8

For the cheesecake, wrap the tofu in plenty of paper towels and compress under a heavy kitchen utensil for 30 minutes to remove excess water.

Preheat the oven to 180°C (350°F) Gas 4.

For the cheesecake base, crush the biscuits/crackers to fine crumbs in a food processor or blender by putting them into a resealable bag and bashing them with a rolling pin. Transfer the crumbs to a mixing bowl and stir in the melted butter and cinnamon until well combined. Spread the biscuit/cracker mixture evenly over the bottom of the cake pan and press down to flatten.

Combine the tofu and soft cheese in the rinsed out food processor or blender, and blend to combine. Transfer to a bowl and add the sugar, eggs, lemon zest and vanilla seeds. Mix well until all the ingredients are evenly combined. Pour the mixture over the top of the biscuit/cracker base.

Bake in the preheated oven for 10 minutes, then reduce the oven temperature to 160°C (325°F) Gas 3 and bake for a further 45–50 minutes.

Turn the oven off and allow the cheesecake to cool completely for 2–3 hours in the oven, which should help stop cracks from forming. Then remove from the oven and leave at room temperature for a few hours before transferring to the refrigerator and chilling overnight.

The next day, remove the cheesecake from its pan, transfer to a serving plate and scatter fresh berries on top to serve.

MANGO SMOOTHIE

MANGOES ARE A TROPICAL FRUIT WHICH GROW IN PLENTY OF SUNSHINE; THEREFORE MANY SOUTHEAST ASIANS BELIEVE THEY ARE VERY WARMING TO THE BODY AND HENCE EATING TOO MANY CAN LEAVE YOU WITH A SORE THROAT AND A RESTLESS NIGHT'S SLEEP – SO MANGOES SHOULD BE EATEN IN MODERATION!

2 ripe mangoes
250 ml/1 cup natural/plain yogurt
4 tablespoons condensed milk

SERVES 2–4

Peel and chop the mangoes into pieces, then blend together with the yogurt, 500 ml/2 cups water and the condensed milk until smooth. Serve immediately.

VARIATION: MANGO LASSI ICE CREAM
Follow the recipe as above then churn in an ice cream maker for 50 minutes. Freeze for at least 4 hours. Makes 1 litre/1 quart.

STICKY RICE WITH MANGO *(right)*

STICKY RICE WITH MANGO (KHAO NIEW MAMUANG) IS PROBABLY THAILAND'S FAVOURITE SWEET DISH. MANY WILL EVEN ASK IF IT IS AVAILABLE ON A MENU BEFORE ORDERING THEIR MAIN COURSES. REMEMBER THAT STICKY RICE MUST BE SOAKED FOR AT LEAST 3 HOURS OR OVERNIGHT.

400 g/2 cups volume sticky rice
300 ml/1¼ cups coconut milk
2 tablespoons caster/granulated sugar

½ teaspoon salt
4 ripe mangoes
2 tablespoons coconut cream, to serve

SERVES 4

Soak and cook the sticky rice according to packet instructions and use while still warm.

Put the coconut milk and sugar in a small saucepan and heat gently, stirring all the time, until the sugar has dissolved. Do not let boil.

Stir in the salt and the warm sticky rice and set aside.

To prepare the mangoes, cut the 2 cheeks off each one, as close to the stone/pit as possible. Cut each cheek into 4–6 long wedges, cutting through the flesh but not through the skin. Peel back and discard the skin.

Pile a mound of sticky rice in the centre of a serving dish and arrange the slices of mango around it. Pour the coconut cream over the rice and serve warm or cold. Alternatively, serve the rice in small bowls, add a few slices of mango, then trickle the coconut cream over the top.

BANANA FRITTERS
WITH COCONUT CUSTARD

BANANAS ARE THE MOST IMPORTANT TRADITIONAL FRUIT OF VIETNAM. THEY
ARE GROWN AND SOLD EVERYWHERE AND USED IN MANY DESSERT DISHES.
JUST-RIPE BANANAS WORK BEST WITH THIS RECIPE.

6 ripe bananas

200 g/1½ cups rice flour

1 x 400-ml.14-oz. can
    coconut milk

100 g/½ cup caster/granulated
    sugar

dash of pure vanilla extract
    or **seeds** from 1 vanilla
    pod/bean

4 tablespoons sunflower/
    safflower oil

icing/confectioners' sugar,
    for dusting

COCONUT CUSTARD

1 x 400-ml/14-oz. can
    coconut milk

1 teaspoon salt

1 teaspoon caster/granulated
    sugar

SERVES 6–10

Slice the bananas in half lengthways, then cut them into 7.5-cm/
3-in. pieces.

In a bowl, mix together the rice flour, coconut milk, sugar and
vanilla to create a smooth batter. Add the bananas and mix
to coat with batter.

Heat the oil in a frying pan/skillet on medium heat and shallow
fry the coated banana pieces for about 2–3 minutes on each side
or until golden brown. Set aside on paper towels.

To make the coconut custard, gently heat the coconut milk with
the salt and sugar in a pan until warm.

Serve the fritters warm or at room temperature, dusted with
icing sugar, with the coconut custard.

AVOCADO ICE CREAM

IN SOUTHEAST ASIA, AVOCADOS ARE USUALLY CONSUMED SWEET. AS THEY HAVE A HIGH (MOSTLY MONOUNSATURATED) FAT CONTENT, THEY ARE AN IMPORTANT STAPLE WHERE FATTY FOODS SUCH AS DAIRY, FATTY MEAT AND FISH ARE LIMITED. IN VIETNAM, MANY STREET VENDORS SELL FRUIT JUICES AND SMOOTHIES DAY AND NIGHT (ESPECIALLY AT NIGHT). ONE OF THE MOST POPULAR SMOOTHIES IS AVOCADO WITH SUGAR OR CONDENSED MILK , OR WITH OTHER FRUIT JUICES THAT PAIR WELL LIKE COCONUT OR PAPAYA.

2 ripe avocados
520 ml/2¼ cups coconut water
5 tablespoons condensed milk
a handful of mint leaves, finely chopped, to garnish (optional)

ice cream maker (optional)

SERVES 4–6

Cut the avocados in half and scoop out the flesh, discarding the skin and stones/pits. Blend the flesh together with the coconut water and condensed milk. If you do not have a blender or food processor, mash in a bowl with a potato masher or fork until smooth.

Churn in an ice cream maker for 1 hour (time may vary according to ice cream maker). Freeze for at least 2 hours. If you do not have an ice cream maker, after blending freeze for 2 hours, then blend again; repeat this process at least twice over 2 days. Serve with mint leaves, if desired.

To serve as a shake/smoothie simply put the ingredients in a blender or food processor (with or without ice) and use only 4 tablespoons of condensed milk. If you do not wish to use dairy, sweeten with sugar instead.

HONG KONG EGG TARTS

THESE PASTRIES WERE INTRODUCED TO HONG KONG TEAHOUSES IN THE 1940S
AND HAVE SINCE BECOME A STAPLE IN CHINESE BAKERIES. THEY DIFFER FROM
THE EUROPEAN VERSION IN THE UNIQUE WAY THE PUFF PASTRY IS MADE.

100 g/⅓ cup milk
50 g/¼ cup caster/superfine
   sugar
2 eggs
seeds from 1 vanilla pod/bean

FOR THE WATER DOUGH

100 g/¾ cup Asian white wheat
   flour
15 g/1 heaped tablespoon caster/
   superfine sugar
30 g/2 tablespoons unsalted
   butter, melted

FOR THE BUTTER DOUGH

100 g/¾ cup Asian white wheat
   flour
50 g/3½ tablespoons unsalted
   butter, melted

a round fluted pastry/
   cookie cutter
12 individual mini tart pans

MAKES 12

In a large mixing bowl, combine the water dough ingredients and add 3 tablespoons water. Form into a ball and knead lightly until smooth and silky. Wrap the dough in clingfilm/plastic wrap and chill in the fridge for 15 minutes. Divide the dough into 12 and roll each piece into a ball. Cover with a damp kitchen cloth and set aside.

In a second mixing bowl, repeat the same process with the butter dough ingredients but instead of chilling, rest at room temperature for 15 minutes.

To assemble the dough, take a water dough ball and knead gently and briefly. Very lightly flour the worktop and use a rolling pin to roll out the ball of water dough to a diameter of 7.5 cm/ 3 in. Place a butter dough ball in the centre and wrap the water dough around to enclose it completely. Turn the dough ball over so the join is on the underside. Roll the combined dough into a thick square parcel. Fold the parcel into three and flatten with the rolling pin again. Repeat this fold and roll process twice with each ball. Cover and rest in the fridge for 15 minutes.

Whilst the dough is chilling, make the custard. Whisk together the milk, sugar, eggs and vanilla seeds in a large bowl until the sugar has fully dissolved. Pass the mixture twice through a sieve/ strainer to make sure it is as smooth as possible.

Roll out each chilled dough ball and use a round cutter with a fluted edge to stamp out circles of dough to fit the mini tart pans. Lay a circle of dough in the tart pan and prick the base with a fork. Repeat for all 12 dough balls. Leave the tart pans to chill in the fridge for 5 minutes.

Preheat the oven to 200°C/400°F/Gas 6.

Pour the egg mixture into the tart shells to come three quarters of the way up the sides. Bake in the preheated oven for 10 minutes. Lower the oven temperature to 170°C/325°F/Gas 3 and bake for a further 10 minutes. Leave to cool on a wire rack before serving.

INDEX